beyond METAL

makingmemories

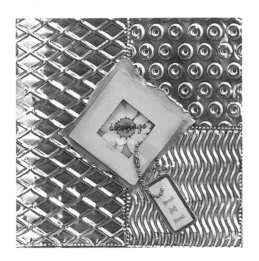

This book is dedicated to **Bridgette Server,** *founder of Making Memories. It is her drive, passion, and love of preserving memories that inspires us to push harder and continually take everything to the next level. We would like to thank her for her strength and her vision.*

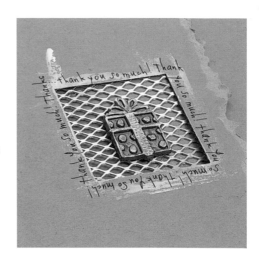

beyond: 1. on the farther side of

2. to a degree or amount greater than

3. in addition to

At Making Memories, we push ourselves beyond obvious limits with every breath. It all started with the introduction of metal Details™. It grew as we responded with more creative and easy-to-use metal accents designed for crafters of all abilities. And it takes on a new life with this introduction of *Beyond Metal,* our first-ever idea book that puts a new twist on the hottest embellishments your fingers have ever touched.

We challenged some of our most celebrated artists to apply their talents in creating these extraordinary pages of ideas. Beyond traditional scrapbooking layouts, we splashed innovation on cards, boxes, books, picture frames, and countless gift projects. We played with ink, paint, embossing powder, and sandpaper to add interest and impact. We even raided hardware stores to find powerful ways to customize the look of metal.

Best of all, we translated these awe-inspiring creations into simple, straightforward recipes so you can astound your family, your friends, and yourself with designer-level artistry.

Set your creative fears aside and open the windows of your imagination. Join us for this look Beyond Metal. be inspired!

alphabet charms

eyelet alphabet

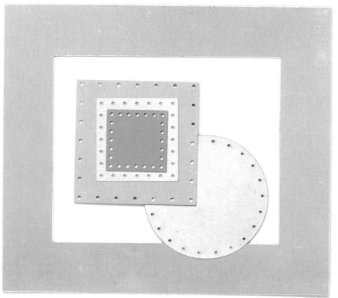
metal frames & stitched tin tiles

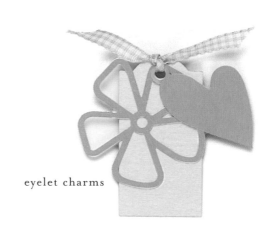
eyelet charms

charmed plaques

eyelet shapes

eyelet tag alphabet

wire words

eyelet letters

metal words

laugh

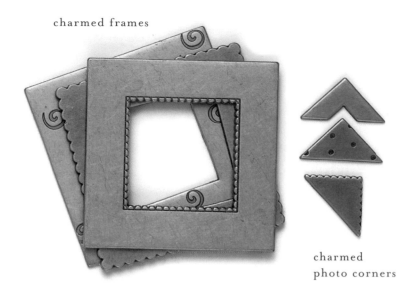

charmed frames

charmed
photo corners

eyelet quotes

eyelet words

imagine

create

eyelet phrases

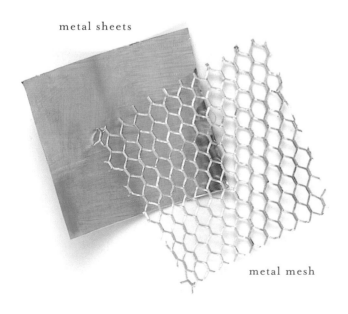

metal sheets

metal mesh

CONTENTS

The metal products showcased in these chapters look great when used "as-is," but you open a whole new window of opportunity when you alter the metal to create customized embellishments. Here are just a few suggestions of how you can alter the pieces and add a personal, artistic flair to your work.

1: Completely paint the Charmed Plaque with acrylic paint, making sure the paint goes into all the indentions. Allow to dry completely. Rub off paint with steel wool until you achieve the desired look.

2: You can alter the color of Eyelet Letters with embossing powder. Hold the letter with tweezers, press it into an embossing or VersaMark inkpad, and dip in powder. Heat emboss with white Ultra Thick Embossing Enamel.

3: Alter metal by covering the pieces with Metal Mesh.

4: Use metal stamps to create impressions in the metal. To emphasize the stamped word, rub acrylic paint into the letters and wipe off the excess with a wet wipe. Try using the Simply Stated Rub-Ons on the metal, as well.

5: Stamp words or images onto metal pieces. To prepare the surface for stamping, completely cover the metal with acrylic paint and allow to dry. You will need to apply 2-3 coats, allowing the paint to dry in between coats. Now you can stamp on it!

6: Holding the eyelet portion of the Eyelet Word with tweezers, press the face of the word on a white inkpad. While the ink is still wet, dip the piece into the clear Ultra Thick Embossing Enamel and heat emboss. Repeat. Try with different colors of ink for a totally different look!

7: It's remarkably easy to cut Eyelet Charms. Use utility scissors or tin snips to fashion whatever shape you need. The long, skinny tag shown here was cut from a large oval Eyelet Charm tag.

8: Cover Metal Words with paper for an interesting look. Apply glue to the word, then press paper on top, making sure it is well adhered. After it is dry, go back with an X-Acto knife and trim around the edges. Cover with a decoupage medium.

9: Change the color of the Eyelet Alphabet by rubbing paint down into the letters or numbers. While the paint is still wet, wipe off the excess with a wet wipe. Try placing a Page Pebble over the numbers for added dimension.

10: The non-porous and hard nature of the metal makes for a perfect decoupage surface. Adhere the flowers with a dab of glue, then brushed Mod Podge over the top. It's also surprisingly easy to drill holes in the metal. With holes in the product, you can hang the metal piece or simply dangle items from wire.

11: The Metal Frames cut easily with scissors. You can change their profile or even cut them at the corners, punch holes, set eyelet, and tie them back together.

12: Give Metal Words a unique color with paint and chalk. First, paint them with white acrylic paint. When dry, apply chalk to the surface.

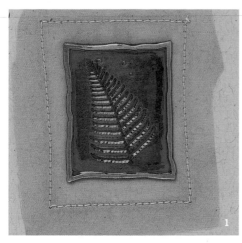

1

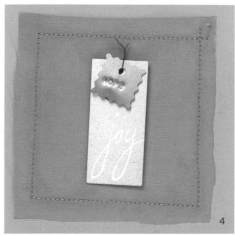

2

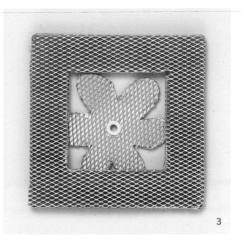

3

4

5

6

7

8

9

10

11

12

1 alphabet charms & eyelet alphabet

At last there is proof that everything you need to know you learned in kindergarten. The alphabet is the most basic element of the human language, but Alphabet Charms™ are anything but basic. Living up to their name by offering a charming assortment of sizes, shapes, fonts, and both uppercase and lowercase letters, Alphabet Charms™ can be mixed and matched to create unique titles and accents. Try layering tiny letters on top of an extra-large letter. Add dimension by raising some letters with Sticky Squares™. Or highlight each letter of a word with a different treatment such as patterned and solid papers, metal-rimmed tags, or Charmed Frames™. Don't be shy—remember the most compelling designs are the ones that combine a mix of everything!

Eyelet Alphabet™ letters are just as fun and striking to use. With their delightfully delicate and artistic finish, you can incorporate these accents into any project. It's as simple as A–B–C. When used alone, they create a clean and simple title. You can sand the surface to reveal a copper color. Or you can add depth by either putting a Page Pebble™ on top or framing them with buttons. However you choose to use these products, you'll earn an A+ for creativity.

1 LOVE WITHOUT MEASURE
By Heidi Swapp

Alphabet charms: Making Memories
Concho: Scrapworks
Measuring tape: Dritz
Paper: Making Memories, Daisy D's,
and K & Company
Tag: American Tag
Other: Chinese coin and ribbon

how to: Last year Heidi started a tradition of photographing her kids with these LOVE letters. To showcase your sweet photos, fold a 2" strip of paper in half and "wrap" it around one side of the layout. Stitch in place. Cut a strip of measuring tape and affix it across your page with double-sided tape. Adhere the Alphabet Charms with Metal Glue, mixing sizes and shapes to get all the letters you need. In the word "love," Heidi substituted a coin for the "o," and she used tiny Alphabet Charms to spell the word "love" on top of the big "L."

2 BABY BOOK
By Heidi Swapp

Adhesive: Perfect Paper, USArtQuest
Eyelet alphabet: Making Memories
Paint: Folk Art
Paper: Making Memories and
Autumn Leaves
Stamps: Club Scrap
Twill snap tape: Scovill
Other: Cardboard and old book paper

how to: Cut a piece of cardboard to desired size. Score a spine on each side, deep enough to accommodate the inside pages. Fold the front flaps over, overlapping them slightly. Cover the inside and outside of the cardboard with paper. Decoupage the outside using Perfect Paper. Stitch on paper accents. Use a rubber stamp inked with acrylic paint to stamp the image onto the front. Sand the edges and various places to age the cover. Sew five 4" x 6" photo sleeves to the inside. To create the closure, set an Eyelet Alphabet letter into each snap on the twill tape. To set the eyelets, Heidi cut through the twill tape on the female side of the snap. Then she inserted the eyelet and set it. The eyelet won't set all the way through, but it'll set enough to hold. Finger paint a bit of cream acrylic paint on each letter, then sand it off a little when dry. The twill tape fits snugly around the book.

3 TIC TAC TOE
By Heidi Swapp

Adhesive: Mod Podge, Plaid
Alphabet charms: Making Memories
CD tin: Impress Rubber Stamps
Patterned paper: Making Memories
and Daisy D's
Silk ribbon: Bucilla
Other: Checked ribbon, magnet sheet,
and shopping bag

how to: Create a personalized travel tic tac toe board in just a few easy steps. First, cover the top of a tin with paper cut from a shopping bag. Then cut nine squares of patterned paper, each with a different pattern. Adhere the paper to the tin and divide each section with ribbon. Frame the outside of the squares with ribbon, as well. Once it is all glued down, coat the entire cover with Mod Podge. Adhere a small magnet sheet to the back of each Alphabet Charm. Store the letters inside when not in use!

4 TRUE LOVE CARD
By Heidi Swapp

Eyelet alphabet, eyelet letters, eyelet words,
shaped clip, and vellum: Making Memories
Paper: Making Memories
Tag: Avery

how to: Create a tri-fold card. On the bottom flap, layer and position Eyelet Letters (LOVE), a torn piece of vellum, and a strip of patterned paper, which is folded over to the back. Lift the back flap of the patterned paper, then set all the pieces with Eyelet Alphabet Letters. Once the eyelets are set, you'll fold and secure the paper in place to cover the backs of the set eyelets. A Shaped Clip holds the card shut.

1

2

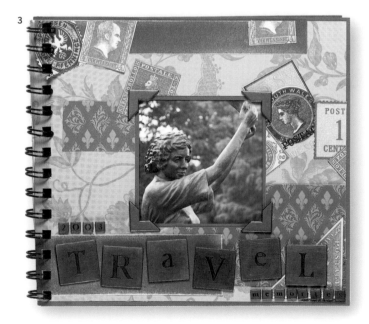

3

1 CELEBRATE FRANKIE TURNING THIRTEEN
By Stephanie McAtee

Alphabet charms, charmed frame, eyelet words, and snaps: Making Memories
Alphabet stamps: PSX Design
Brass flower: Anima Designs
Dried flower: Pressed Petals
Metallic rub-ons: Craf-T Products
Paper: Paper Source
Pen: EK Success
Ribbon and tags: Paper Source
Stamping ink: Memories
Waxed linen: Darice
Other: Brass tag, chipboard, envelope, gold frame, jeweled ponytail, metal alphabet stamps, sheet metal, and Velcro

how to: To support the metal embellishment on the left side, adhere a piece of chipboard to the back of the layout. Use the packing tape transfer technique to lift the zodiac sign (capricorn) from a magazine. Apply a piece of packing tape to an image. Rub over the top with a bone folder to make sure the tape is well adhered. Soak the piece of packing tape with the image stuck to the back in a cup of water for a few minutes. Remove from the water and rub off the paper backing. The image should be transferred to the tape. Blot dry to remove excess water.

Stephanie made a mini-album—with large tags for the pages—so she could accommodate more photos on her layout. On the front of each tag is a photo and the back of each tag is reserved for Frankie to do her own journaling. At the end of each tag, tie a ribbon.

2 SEASONAL TAGS
By Kris Stanger

Alphabet charms and eyelets:
Making Memories
Antique glass beads: Mill Hill
Butterfly rubber stamp: PSX Design
Dried leaves: Nature's Pressed
Flower corners: Jolee's Boutique, Stickopotamus
Mesh: Magenta
Miniature garden tools: Provo Craft
Paper: Making Memories, Memories, Magenta, All About Me Paper Co., and Pebbles in My Pocket
Ribbon: The Card Connection
Snowflake eyelets: The Stamp Doctor
Other: Mulberry paper

how to: Create a tag for every season. Cut your tag first, then set the eyelets. Now have fun embellishing! For the summer tag, Kris suggests penciling in your design before stitching.

3 2003 TRAVEL MEMORIES
By Erin Terrell

Alphabet charms and charmed photo corners: Making Memories
Paper: Making Memories and Anna Griffin
Photo album: Canson

how to: Remove the cover from a pre-made photo album. Cut coordinating patterned papers to fit over the album cover and glue into place. Use low-tack artist's tape to strengthen the binding area of the cover. Open the album so you can see the square holes in the cover. Use an X-Acto knife to cut the paper and tape from the pre-existing holes. Adhere the Alphabet Charms and Charmed Photo Corners to the front of the album. Replace album cover.

4 GIRLS CAMP
By Rhonda Solomon

Alphabet charms, charmed frame, charmed photo corners, eyelets, metal-rimmed tags, and snaps:
Making Memories
Embossing enamel: Ultra Thick Embossing Enamel, Suze Weinberg
Fiber: Timeless Touches
Leaf die cut: Deluxe Designs
Metallic rub-ons: Craf-T Products
Paper: Making Memories
Ribbon: The Trim Shop
Rubber stamps: Hero Arts
Stamping ink: Clearsnap

how to: Rubber stamp background squares on which to mount Alphabet Charms and journaling. Place letters on tags, printed paper, and stamped paper. Attach title to moss-colored cardstock. Rhonda attached parts of her title with eyelets, snaps, and fibers. Print out your journaling on various papers and cardstocks. Re-create the title backgrounds for your journaling mats. Add Charmed Photo Corners, Alphabet Charms, and trim for embellishment. Place photos on the page. The "fossil" was made by placing the metal frame on cardstock, then adding embossing enamel inside and heating. Repeat the embossing step a few times and wait a few seconds. Press into the warm enamel with a rubber stamp. When cool, rub with metallic rub-ons. Add to page along with the leaf die cut.

1 THROUGH THE EYES OF AN ARTIST
By Robin Johnson

Charmed frames, eyelet alphabet, and
page pebbles: Making Memories
Twine: Hillcreek Designs
Other: Aleene's Instant Decoupage Matte

how to: Have your photo enlarged to
5" x 7" and ask for two prints—a color
print and a black and white print. Trim
the photos to size, then tear the center
section out of the color print. Lay the
color photo pieces on top of the black
and white. Use the remaining color
section to cut out and use in another
place on your layout.

Put the adhesive on the front and back
of the leaves. Coating the leaves will
make them softer and more pliable.
Secure in position on your page and
set the Eyelet Alphabet letters on top.
Add a Page Pebble to the top of each
Eyelet Alphabet letter.

2 OUR FAMILY
By Jennifer Jensen

Alphabet stamps: PSX Design
Bead chain, eyelet alphabet,
eyelet word, funky with fibers, and
metal-rimmed tags: Making Memories
Chenille rick rack: Wright
Dog tag and chain: Chronicle Books
Stamping ink: Stampin' Up!
Velveteen paper: Paper Adventures
Other: Denim fabric, flowers, old buttons,
ribbon, safety pins, and screen mesh

how to: Fold an 11" square of
cardboard in half. Cover with two
pieces of 12" x 12" cardstock. Sew
the cardstock together on the sides
and in the crease, encasing the
cardboard. Before stitching, insert
a piece of ribbon on each side to tie
the book closed. Add embellishments.
Jennifer also added fabric pockets to
the inside of her book to hold photos.
Note: Old buttons can be the perfect
"frame" for Eyelet Alphabet letters!

3 PATIENCE
By Jennifer Jensen

Alphabet stamps: PSX Design
Eyelet alphabet, eyelets, and
jump rings: Making Memories
Paper: Making Memories and Magenta
Photo mat: Hunt
Photographs: Legends
Stamping ink: Stampin' Up!
Twine: Ripped from the side of fabric
Other: Buttons and corrugated paper

how to: For the fibers on the page,
Jennifer simply ripped a piece of
brown fabric, then tore several strands
from one side. The mini-book with a
sewn binding contains the journaling
for the layout.

4 CARDS AND ENVELOPES
By Jennifer Jensen

Circle punch: Carl
Eyelet alphabet, eyelets, funky with
fibers, and snaps: Making Memories
Heart bead: Blue Moon
Heart button: Le Bouton
Paper: Making Memories, Paper
Adventures, and K & Company
Other: Chenille strip, fabric,
old buttons, and trim

how to: Keeping with the vintage
theme, Jennifer created cards to
put in the box. Embellish cardstock
cards with raw fabrics, twine, charms,
buttons, and Eyelet Alphabet letters.
Tear pages from old books to make
the insides of the cards.

5 WORDS SHARED
By Jennifer Jensen

Eyelet alphabet and eyelets:
Making Memories
Metal clasp: JHB International
Stamping ink: Stampin' Up!
Velveteen paper: Paper Adventures
Other: Buttons, fabric, trim, and twine

how to: Jennifer created this vintage-
looking stationery box by scoring
and cutting thin cardboard. Then she
added olive-colored paper, eyelets, and
twine to reinforce and hold the corners
together. Measure another piece of
olive-colored cardstock to encase the
box. Adhere the box to the cardstock,
then score and fold the paper around
the box. Embellish with fabric, trim,
buttons, eyelets, and Eyelet Alphabet
letters. Jennifer used buttons and
twine to keep the box closed.

2 metal frames, stitched tin tiles & eyelet charms

Your photos and memorabilia deserve to be in the spotlight. Draw attention to them and beautifully ornament your projects with Metal Frames™. Because they are thin and lightweight, you can use several throughout your work to highlight specific details, images, or words. Whether cut apart and tied back together, backed with screen, used as a frame, or altered with the stroke of a brush, the result will be stunning and chic.

Another inventive element with endless possibilities are Stitched Tin Tiles™. These tiles beg to be adorned with stickers, photos, Page Pebbles™, embossing, or any other innovative medium you can dream up. Once embellished or just left plain, you can stitch thread through the holes or attach a series together to create a distinctive border.

While you are dreaming of possibilities, let your mind also think of all the applications Eyelet Charms™ can inspire. Experiment with the many ways these whisper-thin trinkets can bring life to your work. Take a look at how they can be embossed, stamped with rubber stamps or metal stamps, made into magnets, or used for journaling. With these products, you're sure to catch someone's eye!

1 THE TERRELLS
By Erin Terrell

Alphabet stamps: PSX Design
Eyelet tag alphabet, eyelets, jump rings, metal frames, and metal-rimmed tags: Making Memories
Paper: Making Memories and Paper Fever
Pen: EK Success
Ribbon: Offray
Stamping ink: Memories
Other: Magnet quotation

how to: *Frame outer edges of the page with double-dipped cardstock and sand the edges. Place the cream-colored cardstock and green floral paper on the layout as shown. Before adhering, place a strip of double-dipped cardstock along the top of the patterned paper and roll the edges. Stitch two small triangles of green cardstock to create the photo corners. Lighten the color contrast of your photos and print. Frame your photos with Metal Frames. Journal on vellum tags, add a silver eyelet to the tag, then attach to the frame with ribbon. Knot ribbon along the bottom of the page, then hang Eyelet Tag Alphabet letters from ribbon using jump rings. Stamp the word "the" onto cream cardstock using button alphabet stamps and adhere to your page. Erin's tip: It's easy to hang the Eyelet Tag Alphabet from sheer ribbon with jump rings. Jump rings fit through the tiny holes in the ribbon with no hole punching necessary. To keep the alphabet in place, use an adhesive dot on the back of each one.*

2 DAISY CORRESPONDENCE ALBUM
By Erin Terrell

Adhesive: Mod Podge, Plaid
Buttons, charmed photo corners, eyelet charms, and scrapbook stitches: Making Memories
Embossing powder: Stamp-N-Stuff
Envelope template: ScrapPagerz
Extreme Eyelets: Creative Imaginations
Mesh: Magic Mesh
Paper: Making Memories
Rubber stamps: Stampa Rosa
Stamping inks: Memories, Tsukineko, and Clearsnap
Other: Chipboard and fabric

how to: *Cut two pieces of chipboard to 6" x 6". Use Mod Podge to layer papers on album cover and to the inside. Ink the edges of the yellow paper before adhering it to the chipboard. Sand the paper once it has been glued to the album front. Punch holes along the outer edges of chipboard. Use a VersaMark inkpad and white embossing powder to emboss eyelets and Eyelet Charm. Add mesh to the inside of the flower. Add Scrapbook Stitches to the button, then adhere it to the center of the flower with an adhesive dot. Create the flower petals and green envelope. Rubber stamp script onto cream cardstock, then ink the edges with brown ink. Hang the heart-shaped Eyelet Charm from papers. Set eyelets along the outer edge of album. Tie fabric strips through the eyelets. Erin's tip: Use adhesive dots to adhere items on top of mesh. Also, when embossing, hold metal with rubber-gripped needle-nosed pliers to avoid burning your fingers.*

3 THANK YOU CARD
By Erin Terrell

Alphabet stamps: PSX Design
Beads (large): JewelCraft
Beads, jump rings, metal-rimmed tags, page pebbles, scrapbook stitches, and stitched tin tile: Making Memories
Floral postage stamps: Stampa Rosa
Paper: Making Memories and Paper Adventures
Ribbon: Offray
Stamping inks: Tsukeniko and Fresco

how to: *Form a 6" x 12" card and use a bone-folder to score 3" in on each side. Fold into thirds. Cut two pieces of printed paper to fit on the front of the card. Wrap ribbon around the top of the card and tie. Stamp message onto metal-rimmed tags, then hang tags and decorative beads from the ribbon with jump rings. Stitch along the outer edges of the Stitched Tin Tiles. Cut floral postage stamps to fit under the square Page Pebbles. Stamp over them with an inkpad to tone them down. Peel off the sticky backing to place the newly decorated Page Pebbles on the tiles. Mount the tiles on double-dipped cardstock. Erin's tip: Use three strands of the Scrapbook Stitches to stitch in the tile. It fits easily through the holes.*

4 DAISY FRAME
By Erin Terrell

Adhesive: Mod Podge, Plaid
Beads, buttons, eyelet alphabet, eyelet charms, eyelet quote, eyelets, scrapbook stitches, and wire: Making Memories
Coastal netting: Magic Scraps
Embossing powder: Ranger Industries
Paper: Making Memories
Stamping ink: Tsukineko
Other: Wooden frame

how to: *Use Mod Podge to cover the frame with paper. Let dry, then sand the edges. Hammer Eyelet Alphabet letters into the top of a wooden frame. Wrap netting around the bottom of the frame and through the opening. Use an adhesive dot to adhere the Eyelet Quote to the netting. Heat emboss flower Eyelet Charms with ink and white embossing powder. Stitch through the button centers, then adhere the buttons to flower Eyelet Charms with adhesive dots. Erin's tip: When you decoupage the frame with paper and Mod Podge, be sure to smooth out all the air bubbles before the glue dries. And only attempt to hammer Eyelet Alphabet letters into a frame made of soft wood.*

1

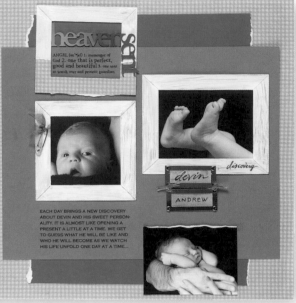

2

3

4

1 FATHER AND SON
By Robin Johnson

Computer fonts: Garamouche, P22;
Copperplate Gothic
Eyelet charms, eyelet letters, metal words,
metal frames, safety pins, and snaps:
Making Memories
Paint: Delta
Paper: Daisy D's and Ka!
Photography: Allison Tyler-Jones
Other: Label and twine

how to: *For the paper-wrapped frame,
cover the bottom portion of a Metal
Frame with paper. Turn the frame
over, and with an X-Acto knife, cut
along the inside edges. Fold the flap
down and glue to the back of the
frame. Other frames are painted
with acrylic paint. Robin used an
X-Acto knife to scrape across the
corners to look like seams. For
the word "father," Robin reversed
the text out of a black box and
printed it on green paper.*

2 KEY TO MY HEART
By Rhonda Solomon

Embossing enamel: Ultra Thick
Embossing Enamel, Suze Weinberg
Metal frame, page pebbles, and snaps:
Making Memories
Paper: Making Memories
Photo corners: Boston International Inc.
Rubber stamps: Rubber Monger
Stamping inks: Clearsnap
Twine: Timeless Touches
Other: Fiber

how to: *Make a book with cardstock and
bind with fiber. Place screw snaps on
the corners of the Metal Frame and
place the frame on the book cover with
pop-up squares. Add a photo to the
inside. Heat emboss key, lock, and
Shakespeare quotation, which were
rubber stamped or printed on vellum.
Add the embellishments to the layout
with a glue pen, fiber, and snaps.*

3 MOMMY KISSES
By Jennifer Jensen

Adhesive: Mod Podge, Plaid
Computer font: CK Newsprint,
Creating Keepsakes
Eyelets, metal frames, metal-rimmed
tags, scrapbook stitches, and snaps:
Making Memories
Paint: Delta
Paper: Making Memories
Other: Blue mesh, buttons, chenille
fabric, and mat board

how to: *For the metal corners, rub
antique paint on a Metal Frame, then
cut them diagonally in the corners.
Sew them back together with snaps
and Scrapbook Stitches. Mount the
photos on mat board and sew a piece
of clear vinyl over the top. Jennifer
cut the letters from a 1958* House
Beautiful *magazine, then decoupaged
a piece of plastic on the top. Make
small tags from mat board and cut
letters from a magazine to put on
top. Print your journaling on old
journal paper and showcase them
in metal-rimmed tags.*

4 METAL FRAMES
By Heidi Swapp

Bead chain, eyelets, metal frames, metal
word, and straight pins: Making Memories
Other: Ribbon and screen

how to: *Cut a piece of screen to the size
of each Metal Frame. Punch holes in all
four corners of each frame. Attach the
screen to the back of the Metal Frame
with eyelets. Punch your photos with
square and circle punches. Pin the
photos to the screen with tiny straight
pins. Heidi also pinned little handwritten
captions to the screen. To attach the
frames to each other, make little bead
chain loops and connect the ends
together. Use a 9" length of bead chain
to create a "hanger" for the top. Attach
the "family" Metal Word with adhesive
dots to the bottom of the last frame.*

1 CHOOSE THE BETTER PART
By Lynne Montgomery

Buttons, page pebble, stitched tin tiles:
Making Memories
Computer fonts: Kids, Microsoft Works;
CK Script, *Creating Keepsakes*
Paper: Liz King, EK Success
Photo corners: Boston International Inc.
Tag: American Tag Co.
Other: Embroidery floss, fiber, screen, small
square punch, and thread

how to: *Tear patterned paper diagonally
and adhere it to the bottom of your
background cardstock. Cut a piece of
burlap at a diagonal, fray the top edge,
and adhere it to the patterned paper.
Place a small piece of screen diagonally
in the bottom corner of your page,
opposite of the burlap corner. Repeat
the same process (minus the screen)
on the top right corner of your layout.
To create the Stitched Tin Tile border,
tie embroidery floss through the button
holes. Use an adhesive dot to attach the
buttons to the tiles. Punch your page
title with a square punch, adhere it to
one of the tiles, then adhere a square
Page Pebble over the title for added
depth. Thread the tiles together with
fiber. Lay them out across the bottom of
your page and glue down. Wrap the ends
of the fiber around to the back of your
page. Lay a heavy book over the glued
tiles to hold them in place while drying.
Create photo mat and journaling block.
Machine stitch around the edges of
the entire layout. Lynne's tip: Back
the entire layout with an additional
piece of cardstock before stitching it,
sandwiching in the wire screen that
was wrapped around the corners to
prevent the screen from catching.*

2 NATURE
By Lynne Montgomery

Embossing enamel: Ultra Thick Embossing
Enamel, Suze Weinberg
Eyelets, metal-rimmed tag, and
stitched tin tile: Making Memories
Flower rubber stamp: PSX Design
Hemp: Darice
Paper: Liz King, EK Success
Stamping inks: Tsukineko and Hero Arts
Twine: May Arts
Walnut ink: Postmodern Design
Other: Burlap, dictionary definition,
embossed chipboard, and packing tape

how to: *Brush a piece of chipboard with
walnut ink. Allow to dry. Apply an inkpad
directly to a Stitched Tin Tile, sprinkle
with embossing enamel, and heat-set.
Let cool and repeat two or three more
times. On the last time, while the
enamel is still molten, press an inked
rubber stamp into the enamel. Hold
for a few seconds, then remove. Lynne
used the packing tape image transfer
technique (see chapter 1) to put
the definition on the vellum. Cut the
transferred image to the size of your
vellum tag. The image should still be a
little sticky and shouldn't need adhesive.
Adhere a torn piece of patterned paper to
the tag. Add the Stitched Tin Tile with
eyelets and twine. Lynne's tip: If you're
planning to stitch through the holes of
the Stitched Tin Tile after you've com-
pleted your embossed image, make sure
you clear the enamel away from the
holes by poking a needle though each
hole while the enamel is still warm.*

3 ZIP ON OVER
By Lynne Montgomery

Computer fonts: CK Script, CK Wanted,
and CK Constitution, *Creating Keepsakes*
Embroidery floss: DMC
Eyelets and stitched tin tile:
Making Memories
Paper: Provo Craft
Pressed flower: Pressed Petals
Stamping ink: Clearsnap
Other: Burlap, rubber stamp, tag,
transparency, and zipper

how to: *Cut a piece of burlap to approximately 4" x 5". In the center, cut a slit
3/4" of the way down and hand stitch
a zipper in the slit. Fold a piece of
cardstock in half and crease the fold
with a bone folder. While folded, cut
cardstock approximately 4 1/2" wide and
5 1/2" long. Attach burlap to the front of
the card with eyelets. Cut a smaller
square of cardstock so it will slip down
behind the burlap (in between the eyelets and underneath the zipper). With an
adhesive dot, adhere a pressed flower to
a Stitched Tin Tile. Adhere the tile to
the center of the cardstock insert. Copy
a title onto a transparency and
tear the transparency to fit over the tile.
Hand stitch the cardstock, tin tile, and
transparency together. Slip the cardstock
embellishment behind the burlap and
adhere in place. Cut a piece of patterned
paper to approximately 4" x 5" and
adhere it to the inside of the card. Type
invitation details on a transparency.
Attach it over the patterned paper with
eyelets. Lynne's tip: Transparencies work
great over dried flowers. It protects them
when they're handled.*

4 AFTER HAPPILY EVER AFTER
By Lynne Montgomery

Alphabet charms, eyelet letters, eyelets,
metal-rimmed tags, and stitched tin tile:
Making Memories
Alphabet stamps: PSX Design
Buttons: Jesse James & Co.
Chain: Coffee Break Design
Circle punches: Family Treasures
Computer fonts: Teletype and Bazooka,
Microsoft Works; CK Calligraphy and CK
Constitution, *Creating Keepsakes*
Heart accent: Jolee's Boutique,
Stickopotamus
Label holder: Anima Designs
Paper: Liz King, EK Success; Provo Craft
Stamping ink: Ranger Industries
Sticker: Mrs. Grossman's
Tag punch: Woodward Craft Collection
Tags: American Tag Co.
Other: Chipboard, embroidery floss, envelope,
fiber, glass beads, hemp, and safety pin

how to: *Cut a front and back cover
from chipboard. Cover chipboard with
decorative paper, wrapping the edges to
the inside. For the cover embellishment,
use a non-porous ink to stamp the title
onto the tin tile. Add eyelets and tie
the burlap to the cover with embroidery
floss. The spine of the book is folded
accordion style just like a paper fan would
be folded. Cut two pieces of paper to
12" x 4 1/2" and use spray adhesive to
adhere the two pieces of paper together.
When you fold those papers accordion
style, you'll have a pattern on both
sides. Fold the paper back and forth
until the entire strip is folded. Cut off
the top portion of long, rectangular
envelopes to make 4 1/2" tall "pocket
pages." Cut windows in the front of
each envelope with an X-Acto knife,
then cut a notch out of the top using
a circle punch. Attach an envelope to
the right side of each accordion fold
with a strip of photo tape. Adhere the
accordion binding to the chipboard
covers. (One end should be attached
to the inside front cover and one end
attached to the inside back cover.)
Cover the raw edges on the inside of
the cover with decorative paper. Tie the
book closed with hemp.*

4b

1a

1b

1 SECOND ANNIVERSARY CARD
By Heidi Swapp

Alphabet stamps: PSX Design and
Inkadinkado
Defined stickers, eyelet charms, eyelets,
metal-rimmed tags and staples:
Making Memories
Fibers: On the Surface
Modeling paste: Liquitex
Walnut ink: Postmodern Design
Watercolors: Peerless
Other: Hair elastic, hemp, #2 from a
bingo card, old book paper, safety pin,
and various rubber stamps

how to: *Smear modeling paste onto the
tag Eyelet Charms and allow to dry.
Watercolor when dry. Tie tags and fibers
to hemp. Set eyelets in the top and
bottom of the card. Tie hemp through
the eyelets. Rubber stamp as desired on
tags over the modeling paste. Stitch a
border of book paper on the edge of the
card. Staple a long, skinny definition on
the right side of the card. Stamp the
word "anniversary" along the book
paper. To keep the card closed, put a
hair elastic around it. Since it was the
recipients' second anniversary, Heidi cut
a little "2" from a bingo card and safety
pinned it to the elastic band.*

*For the inside, wrap book paper and
a ribbon around the main photo. Attach
a walnut-inked tag to the ribbon. Include
another Defined Sticker under the
other photos.*

2 BROTHERLY LOVE
By Robin Johnson

Buttons: Cousin Corp.
Defined sticker, eyelet charms,
and snaps: Making Memories
Fiber: EK Success
Paper: Making Memories
Screen: Scrapworks
Tags: Avery
Other: Dried flower

how to: *Use Page Pebbles to accentuate
small dried flowers. To make the embellishment, lightly glue small dried flowers
to the top of a round Eyelet Charm.
Use a leaf or petal to cover the hole in
the Eyelet Charm. Put a Page Pebble
on top. Robin also spruced up Eyelet
Charms by "matting" them with solid or
patterned paper, such as on the heart
Eyelet Charm. You could also put paper
on top of the charm for journaling or you
could tear photos a little smaller than
the Eyelet Charm and apply to the top
to achieve a metal-rimmed look. Stitch
across photos to hold them in place.
Robin's tip: Try using a color photo as
an added highlight while using black
and white for your other photos.*

3 REMINISCE, ADVENTURE, COMMITMENT, MEMORIES
By Emily Waters

Alphabet stamps: The Missing Link
Stamp Company
Defined stickers, eyelets, jump rings,
scrapbook stitches, and stitched tin tiles:
Making Memories
Paper: Making Memories and Daisy D's
Stamping ink: Anna Griffin
Other: Metal stamps and ribbon

how to: *Create pockets along the bottom
by sewing around the outsides and up a
3" x 12" strip of oatmeal cardstock.
Attach photos to large Stitched Tin Tiles
and sew around them using a zigzag
stitch. Use metal stamps to stamp the
names into the small Stitched Tin Tiles,
then attach the tiles together with jump
rings. Create the tops of tags by placing
small Stitched Tin Tiles at the top. Use
a hole punch to create a hole in the tile
and set an eyelet. Place ribbon through
the hole. To use Stitched Tin Tiles as a
photo holder, place the tile half on and
half off your photo. Stitch around half of
the tile, then fold tile in half around to
the back of your photo mat. Follow the
same technique using desired stitching
to create title holders.*

2

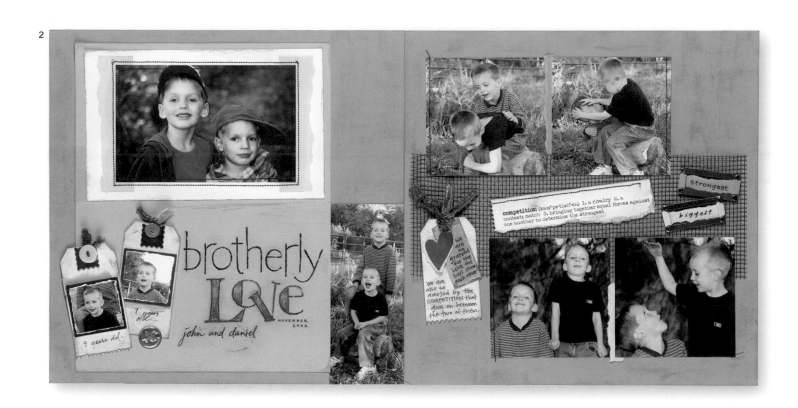

brotherly LOVE

NOVEMBER 2002

john and daniel

4 years old...

7 years old...

competition (kom'petish'en) 1. a rivalry 2. a contest match 3. bringing together equal forces against one another to determine the strongest

strongest

biggest

We are so grateful for the love the boys show each other.

We are also so amused by the COMPETITION that goes on between the two of them.

3

[rem·in·isce]
to think about, usually with fondness

[ad·ven·ture]
an unusual, exciting, often romantic experience

[com·mit·ment]
TO DEDICATE ONESELF TO SOMETHING OR SOMEONE

[mem·or·ies]
that which is retained in memory; things past

1 TAG SERIES
By Stephanie McAtee

Alphabet stamps: PSX Design
Brass flower: Anima Designs
Calligraphy nib: Manto Fev
Computer font: Old Typewriter,
downloaded from the Internet
Dog tags: Chronicle Books
Dried flowers: Pressed Petals
Eyelets, eyelet alphabet, eyelet
charms, eyelet words, shapes, snaps,
and staples: Making Memories
Glassine envelope: Paper Source
Journey definition rubber stamp:
Limited Edition Rubber Stamps
Labels: Above the Mark, Limited Edition
Metallic rub-ons: Craf-T Products
Mini-label: Manto Fev
Nail head: Scrapbooker's Dream
Packing tape: 3M
Paper: Making Memories, Frances Meyer,
Paper Source, Seven Gypsies
Ribbon: Paper Source
Stamping ink: Memories
Typewriter rubber stamp: Junque
Waxed linen: Darice
Other: Button, chipboard, conversation
heart candy, clip-on ring, date rubber stamp,
French writing rubber stamp, galvanized
steel, magnets, metal alphabet stamps,
patterned paper, postal and date rubber
stamps, seashells, tiny plastic bag, twine,
vocabulary sticky note

Travel journal tag how to: *Covering the
top of a chipboard tag with travel related
paper makes the perfect backdrop for a
travel tag. To punch a hole in galvanized
steel, use a pointed-end screw or large
nail, and on a wooden, sturdy surface,
use a hammer to make the hole.*

Granddad tag how to: *Personalize
your tags with family photos and add
journaling to describe the subject(s)
of the photos. Give the tag an aged
look with metallic rub-ons.*

Time tag how to: *The clock embellishment is made using the packing tape
transfer technique (see chapter 1).
Apply clear-drying glue to the back of
the transferred image, then place it
on your tag. Smooth and let dry.*

Quintessence tag how to: *Make holes at
the bottom of a chipboard tag with a
paper piercer. Thread a piece of twine
through the dog tag and through the
hole at the bottom of the tag. Tie in a
knot, allowing the dog tag to dangle.
(Tag idea: From Mary Engelbreit's
Home Companion magazine)*

Write tag how to: *Use related items to
make a mini-collage on a tag. Idea to
note: Stephanie wrapped a glassine
envelope around one edge of her tag
and stapled it in place. The envelope
created a nice pocket for another tag.*

Valentine tag how to: *Cut galvanized steel
into a tag shape with metal cutters. Sand
the edges with medium-grain sandpaper
to get rid of any sharp edges. Apply self-
adhesive magnets to the back of the heart
candy and tag Eyelet Charm. Stick them
to the embellished steel. Stephanie's tip:
Work carefully with the galvanized steel
when you cut it, and immediately sand
all freshly-cut edges.*

2 OCEANSIDE DINING
By Heidi Swapp

Alphabet stamps: PSX Design
Brads and eyelet charms:
Making Memories
Embossing enamel: Ultra Thick
Embossing Enamel, Suze Weinberg
Paint: Plaid
Paper: Making Memories
Photo corners: Kolo
Ribbon: May Arts
Other: Book paper

how to: *Paint tag and flower Eyelet
Charms with two coats of acrylic paint,
letting them dry between coats. Once
they are completely dry, carefully sand
the edges so the metal is visible. Now
you can write or stamp on the painted
surface. Press the painted side down
onto a VersaMark inkpad, then dip into
embossing enamel by holding the Eyelet
Charms with tweezers. Heat emboss.
Repeat again for complete coverage.
Heidi's tip: If you don't have the right
color of paint, you can mix colors. The
peach color is about four colors mixed.
Heidi just kept adding paint until she
got the color she wanted!*

3 STAR CHARM CARD
By Heidi Swapp

Chalk: Craf-T Products
Defined stickers, eyelet charm, shaped
clip, and staples: Making Memories
Paint: Folk Art
Other: Ribbon

how to: *Rough up each star Eyelet
Charm with sandpaper. Back the open
stars with vellum and write words on
the vellum. Cut five 3" pieces of ribbon.
Hang the charm in the middle of the
ribbon and machine stitch it to a
rectangle piece of cardstock. Heidi
altered the Defined Sticker by adding
chalk. Attach the sticker to the
cardstock with staples. She altered
another word with paint and attached
it with a Shaped Clip. Machine stitch
the embellished rectangle to a card.*

sand · music · friends · food

oceanside dining

what a perfect ending to a
fabulous island weekend! Our
last evening was dinner on the
beach. Everything was so awesome,
we sat on the beach and watched
the full moon disappear into the
ocean...

Shelly, Ron, Carsie
Feb. 2003

FOOD

3a

3b

1

YOU

1. *shining with light*
2. **brilliant in color or sound;** <u>vivid</u> **3. lively & cheerful** 4. *favorable; hopeful* 5. illustrious

*Addison,
I absolutely love how your 7yr.-pictures turned out ...To me they capture...*

2

Greetings

3

Forget Me Not

4

5

3 eyelet shapes & charmed plaques

Just as the charms on a sentimental bracelet tend to commemorate a significant life event, you can similarly add meaning to your projects with Eyelet Shapes™. The shapes can be used as a page border, for the center of a flower, or simply to dress up your project. Don't forget their utilitarian value either! One artist ingeniously created a closure for a box with a heart Eyelet Shape.

Charmed Plaques™ are another element that will add meaning to your masterpiece. The charm they will bring to your art is literal! While the slim, rectangular Charmed Plaques have many themes and patterns already imprinted on them, be sure to change their look once in a while by brushing the surface with acrylic paint or decoupaging sheer fabric on top for a subtle effect. By using different techniques to alter their appearance, you'll have no problem finding the perfect shape or charm to celebrate the theme of your creation.

1 YOU
By Jennifer Jensen

Defined stickers, eyelet shapes, scrapbook stitches, and snaps: Making Memories
Glass photo holders: Connoisseur
Mirror rosette: Elco
Paper: Design Originals
Photo corners: Canson
Photos: Kris Stanger
Other: Daisy trim, fabric, netting, ribbon, and "You" taken from an old book

how to: *Layer paper, netting, and fabric to make the large flower embellishment.*

2 "GREETINGS" CARD
By Jennifer Jensen

Alphabet stamp: PSX Design and Stampa Rosa
Button: Boutons
Charmed plaque, eyelet shape, and snaps: Making Memories
Eiffel Tower image: Print Shop Deluxe
Hinge: Darice
Paper: Making Memories and Design Originals

how to: *Jennifer made the card base from an old book cover. Embellish with various travel items. Glue a rhinestone on a square Eyelet Shape for a unique addition to the front.*

3 HOPE TAG
By Jennifer Jensen

Charmed plaque and eyelet word: Making Memories
Paint: Delta
Paper: Making Memories
Tag: Made from an old book cover
Other: Button and fabric

how to: *Smear acrylic paint over the metal embellishments for a shabby chic look.*

4 FLOWER TAG
By Jennifer Jensen

Charmed plaque and funky with fiber: Making Memories
Daisy ribbon: Hirschberg Schutz & Co.
Tag: Made from an old book cover
Other: Beads, floral paper, and fringe

how to: *Embellish the center of the flowers with beads and rhinestones.*

5 FORGET ME NOT TAG
By Jennifer Jensen

Adhesive: Mod Podge, Plaid
Charmed plaque, eyelet shape, and scrapbook stitches: Making Memories
Gold beads: Magic Scraps
Paper: Design Originals
Ribbon: Offray
Other: Buttons, fabric, and string

how to: *To alter the look of the Charmed Plaque, decoupage gold sheer fabric over the top.*

1 A YOUNG HEART
By Jennifer Jensen

Beads, charmed photo corner, charmed plaque, eyelet shapes, eyelets, jump rings, snaps, and wire: Making Memories
Computer font: Quigley Wiggly
Embossing powder: Stampin' Up!
Hinges: Darice
Large gray beads: Crystal Components
Paper: Making Memories
Ribbon: Offray
Other: Bracelet links, charms, elastic, fabric, foam board, mat board, and textured paper

how to: *Jennifer constructed the box from mat board and covered it—inside and out—with black paper. Add a patchwork decoration to the front. On the inside, add a hinged piece of mat board, which will open to reveal the contents. Her daughter's medal is inside, attached to foam board. Glue a heart Eyelet Shape on the heart Charmed Plaque, making it 3-D and allowing for the elastic to attach to heart shapes on top of the box.*

2 AMERICAN CHILD
By Lynne Montgomery

Charmed plaque, charmed star, eyelets, and shaped clips: Making Memories
Computer fonts: Footlight MT Light, Microsoft Works; CK Constitution, *Creating Keepsakes*
Paper: K & Company
Walnut ink: Postmodern Design
Other: Chicken wire, foam board, and vellum

how to: *Cut two pieces of foam board 1/4" smaller than the sheet protectors in which they will be stored. With a metal-edged ruler and an X-Acto knife, cut out the entire center from one of the pieces, leaving a 5/8" border on all sides. In the other piece, cut a vertical rectangular window down one side. Using wire cutters, cut chicken wire a bit larger than the foam board openings. Stick the ends of the wire into the foam board. No adhesive is needed. Using photo tape, adhere decorative paper to the back of the foam board so it shows through the chicken wire. Lynne printed song lyrics and journaling on a piece of vellum and placed it over the patriotic paper. Cover the top of the foam board with cardstock, cutting holes in the paper to correspond with the holes in the foam board. Lynne made the holes in her cardstock slightly larger than the foam board cutouts to reduce the visibility of the foam board. If you're planning to have your title wrap around the edge of the border like Lynne's "american child" title, attach the title with eyelets before adhering the cardstock to foam board frame.*

3 ELEMENTAL CHILL
By Stephanie McAtee

Adhesive: Diamond Glaze, JudiKins
Alphabet stamps: PSX Design
Charmed plaque, eyelet alphabet, and staples: Making Memories
Computer font: Old Typewriter, downloaded from the Internet
Definition sticker: Paper Source
Journey definition rubber stamp: Limited Edition Rubber Stamps
Packing tape: 3M
Paper: Making Memories and Bazzill
Walnut ink: Anima Designs
Watch face: Seven Gypsies
Waxed linen: Darice
Other: Chipboard, concho, date stamp, duct tape, envelope, galvanized steel, library pocket, lie detector charm, magnet sheet, metal tag, silver metal frame, and tag

how to: *For the left side of the layout, cover a piece of chipboard with black duct tape. Make and attach a mini-album to the covered chipboard. Stephanie bound the mini-book right onto the layout so it's fully attached. On the right side of the layout, Stephanie wanted to incorporate what's most important to Ethan right now and what he spends a lot of his time doing at this age. To accomplish this goal, she used the packing tape transfer technique to get definitions from an old book (see chapter 1). She also tucked a note to Ethan inside a mini-envelope. At the top of the note is his football number framed by a concho and covered with Diamond Glaze.*

1

1 BOUQUET
By Rhonda Solomon

Buttons, charmed photo corners, eyelet charm, eyelet shapes, and snaps: Making Memories
Garden tools: Darice
Paint: Delta
Ribbon: Timeless Touches
Stamping ink: Marvy Uchida
Thread: Coats & Clark
Other: Alphabet stamps

how to: *For the frame, dry brush aqua cardstock with white paint and a large stippling brush. Miter the corners of the mat and shadow with black ink. Add "nails" by using snaps. Mat on black cardstock. Stamp your title and mat. On the right-hand page, dry brush over journaling for an aged look.*

2 FLOWER SERIES
By Heidi Swapp

Alphabet stamps: Inkadinkado
Embroidery floss: DMC
Eyelet shapes and jump ring: Making Memories
Paint: Folk Art
Other: book rings, box, cardboard, chipboard, ribbon, silk flower, and trim

Flower journal how to: *Cut several sheets of cardstock into quarter-sheet size. Punch two holes in each for the rings to go through, making a book. Cut two pieces of cardboard to make the front and back cover. Punch a hole for the center of the flower and set with an Eyelet Shape.*

Pocket card how to: *The card is folded in thirds and glued in the back. Be sure to affix the flower and ribbon stem before gluing the card together. You could slip a smaller card or tag into this pocket card.*

Blue flower card how to: *Bind two pieces of cardboard with embroidery floss. Embellish with a silk flower, ribbon, and an Eyelet Shape for the center of the flower.*

Flower box how to: *Paint a box with acrylic paint. Turn the box lid upside down and use an anywhere punch to create the hole. Set the flower in place with a round Eyelet Shape. Add ribbon for the stem and an Eyelet Shape for the leaf.*

3 GOBLIN VALLEY
By Robin Johnson

Alphabet charms and eyelet shapes: Making Memories
Fiber: EK Success
Paint: Delta
Paper: Making Memories
Other: Map and sandpaper

how to: *Dry brush the Alphabet Charms with paint. Do a few layers if necessary to get the color you want. Hold the paintbrush flat, instead of at an angle, to avoid filling the letters in with paint. If the letters get filled in, wipe out what you can with a Q-tip and cover the residue with a black marker. To treat the photo edges, sand with a course sandpaper. Rub extra along the edge of the photo to sand it down to white edges.*

4 THE LITTLE LAD WHO DARED TO DREAM BIG
By Erin Terrell

Alphabet stamps: PSX Design
Circle Colluzzle: Provo Craft
Computer fonts: Carpenter ICG and Geeves; Scrap Rhapsody, Lettering Delights Vol. 2
Defined sticker and eyelet shapes: Making Memories
Paper: Making Memories and Provo Craft
Photo paper: Photo Printasia Photo Satin Paper, Ilford
Stamping inks: Clearsnap
Vellum: The Paper Company

how to: *Scan and enlarge heritage photos in Photoshop and print. Use an X-Acto knife to cut shapes in the photos, then cut a smaller opening in a piece of blue paper to use as matting. Set the star and football Eyelet Shapes in the window. Stamp "the," "who," and "to" in the title and glue to the layout. Print the title in reverse and cut out with an X-Acto knife. Erin's tip: Make sure to use double prints if you're going to be cutting into the photos.*

2

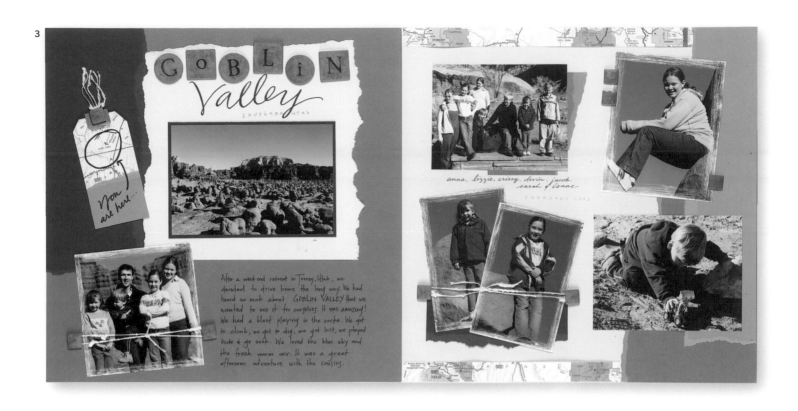

GOBLIN Valley
southern utah

you are here...

After a week-end retreat in Torrey, Utah, we decided to drive home the long way. We had heard so much about GOBLIN VALLEY that we wanted to see it for ourselves. It was amazing! We had a blast playing in the rocks. We got to climb, we got to dig, we got lost, we played hide & go seek. We loved the blue sky and the fresh warm air. It was a great afternoon adventure with the cousins.

anna, lizzie, crissy, devin, jacob, sarah & isaac

the *little lad* who *dared* to *dream* **BIG**

When a little dreamer! Dad tells me that he always dreamed of being a football or a basketball player when he was a child. I guess he got to see out his dreams when he got to high school and college. He spent years playing both soccer and played basketball occasionally with some of his lifelong friends. These photos were taken around 1950 or so.

Erin says: These are some of my favorite photos of you! I love to look at them and try to imagine what you were like as a little kid. I can just picture you running around with all of your football gear on pretending to be the world's best running back or racing your pencil around as Gene Autry!

DREAM 1. a daydream 2. images passing through a sleeping person's mind 3. *to* search and seek out

When you weren't busy being a football star, your other hobby was playing cowboys and Indians. Buddy said you could win fights the cowboys and Indians in your dreams! You saw every cowboy movie the minute it came to town. Lash Larue, Roy Rogers, Hopalong Cassidy, and Gene Autry were the best!

dream

Sarah,
You are
my WISH
come true! I
DREAMED
of a sweet little
girl - and I
got you!

NOVEMBER 2000

Mt Graham

ARIZONA

wish

1

DEVIN

2

Sarah
treasure

imagine

3

4

LIVE
well,
LAUGH
often
LOVE
much...

5

4 eyelet tag alphabet, eyelet letters, metal words & wire words

Confucius once said, "Life is really simple, but we insist on making it complicated." Can't the same be said about our scrapbook pages and projects? Don't make things more complicated than they need to be. By using pre-made words and letters, a complicated-looking project is made simple.

Observe how easily you can dangle Eyelet Tag Alphabet™ letters from a photo or a tag. You can even trim off the sides, creating a whole new shape of letters. While you're trimming the sides off Eyelet Tag Alphabet™ letters, trim the tops off Eyelet Letters™ and adhere them to a layout. Be sure to mix and match the styles of letters for a unique look.

Metal Words™ and Wire Words™ have just as many uses. Paint Metal Words, cut them apart for added emphasis, or attach several together to make a frame. And don't just use Wire Words for accent words; attach a chain to either side of a word to fashion a wearable work of art. No matter how you use these products, only you'll know how simply your artistic venture was created.

1 MY DREAM AND WISH
By Robin Johnson

Adhesive: Perfect Paper, USArtQuest
Eyelet charms, metal-rimmed tags, and metal words: Making Memories
Mesh: Magenta
Paint: Delta
Paper: Making Memories
Ribbon: Hirschberg Schutz & Co., and Offray
Ribbon corners: Anna Griffin
Other: Bead and charm

how to: *Paint Metal Words and flower Eyelet Charm with a coat of white paint. When the paint dries, add a layer of Perfect Paper to act as a fixative for the paint. To make the mesh tag, turn a regular tag over and cut out the vellum with an X-Acto knife. Cut a piece of mesh to the size of your tag. Glue the mesh onto the back metal rim with Metal Glue.*

2 DEVIN TREASURE BOX
By Robin Johnson

Adhesive: Perfect Paper, USArtQuest
Eyelet charms and eyelet letters: Making Memories
Paint: Delta
Paper: Making Memories
Stamping Ink: Tsukineko
Other: Box and twine

how to: *Cover the bottom portion of a box with paper. Sand all the edges. Cut off the corners of a tag Eyelet Charm. You will get two corners from each charm, so cut two charms. Glue these down as corner pieces. Next, glue down the letters. Fold a tag Eyelet Charm in half and glue it to the top to look like a latch. When all pieces are adhered, paint over everything, including the metal. Allow the paint to dry thoroughly. Press a silver inkpad lightly over the top of the metal pieces. This will highlight the metal without coating the background. When finished, complete the box with a coat of Perfect Paper to act as a fixative. Tie twine in the hole of the tag Eyelet Charm.*

3 SARAH TREASURE BOX
By Robin Johnson

Alphabet Stamps: PSX Design
Eyelet letters and eyelet charm: Making Memories
Paint: Delta
Paper: Making Memories
Ribbon: Offray
Stamping Ink: Tsukineko
Other: Box

how to: *Cover the bottom portion of a box with paper. Paint the lid with craft paint. Sand all the edges. Punch a second hole in a tag Eyelet Charm. Tie ribbons in the holes. Glue down the charm and Eyelet Letters to the lid with Metal Glue.*

4 IMAGINE NECKLACE
By Robin Johnson

Beads: Designs by Pamela
Wire and wire word: Making Memories
Other: Chain

how to: *Cut the necklace chain in the center. Cut two 2" pieces of wire. Loop one end of the wire through the "i" of the Wire Word and twist it closed. Add beads to the wire. Loop the other end of the wire through one end of the chain. Twist it closed and cut off the excess. Loop the other wire through the "e" and repeat the process. Make sure there is a clasp on the chain so the word does not get stretched as it is put on.*

5 LIVE, LAUGH, LOVE
By Robin Johnson

Brads: Karen Foster Design
Eyelet letters, eyelet tag alphabet, and staples: Making Memories
Watercolor paper: Strathmore
Watercolors: Crayola

how to: *Cut cardstock to desired size and fold in half. Set aside. Tear a sheet of watercolor paper to fit on the front of the card. Leave a small border around the watercolor paper. Using a brush, cover the entire piece of watercolor paper with water. Add blue paint to the top portion. Change the color to purple and paint the middle section, then switch back to blue to paint the bottom. Dab the watercolor wash softly with a tissue to add a textured look. While the paint is still damp, use the back end of a paintbrush and write words randomly on the paper. The paper will darken where it has been "scratched." Position the metal letters. Use staples to attach the Eyelet Tag Alphabet. Cut off eyelet holes on the Eyelet Letters and adhere with Metal Glue. Leave the eyelet hole on the "O" and the "E." Attach those two letters with brads. When the letters are secure, add the rest of the text with markers. Use a black marker for the main words, and use pastel purple and blue to add more subtle layers of type.*

2

1 QUINCY BABY
By Heidi Swapp

Eyelet tag alphabet and eyelets:
Making Memories
Paper: Making Memories and Seven Gypsies
Ribbon: May Arts and Offray
Other: Glassine envelope

how to: *Heidi changed the shape of the Eyelet Tag Alphabet by trimming off the sides and bottoms of the circles with metal cutters. Set each tag with an eyelet. For added color, run ribbon through each eyelet. Heidi tied a knot in the end of the ribbon, ran it through the front of one eyelet to the back, then up through the next eyelet, and tied another knot. Follow the same steps for the rest of the letters.*

2 DEUX
By Heidi Swapp

Alphabet stamps: Inkadinkado
Eyelet tag alphabet, eyelet words, and scrapbook stitches: Making Memories
Paper: Making Memories and Seven Gypsies

how to: *Mount a small photo on card-stock, then on a piece of foam board. Layer the matted photo on the 8" x 10" enlargement. Poke holes in the smaller photo and tie the Eyelet Tag Alphabet letters on with Scrapbook Stitches. For a rougher look, scratch the alphabet tags with sandpaper.*

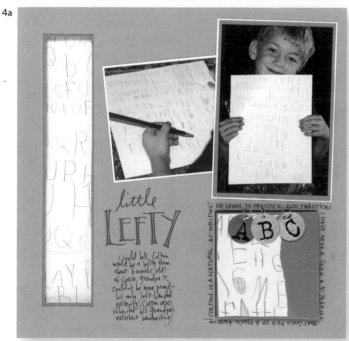

3 PIGTAILS
By Stephanie McAtee

Eyelet tag alphabet, eyelets, and snap:
Making Memories
Grosgrain ribbon: Paper Source
Large metal flower: Anima Designs
Paint: Americana
Paper: Making Memories
Pen: EK Success
Other: Frame hangers, hand-painted sheer
fabric, lingerie ribbon, and photo mat

how to: Cover a piece of 8 1/2" x 11"
cardstock with fabric. Paint the photo
mat pink and let dry. Brush over the
top of the pink with white paint, letting
some of the pink show through. Place
the mat on the fabric, allowing the flowers
on the fabric to be visible through two
of the windows. For the journaling block,
attach a piece of fabric to a piece of
cardstock. Journal on the cardstock, fold
the journaling block in half, and tuck it
underneath a piece of lingerie ribbon.
Attach the Eyelet Tag Alphabet onto the
photo mat with eyelets.

4 LITTLE LEFTY
By Heidi Swapp

Eyelet tag alphabet and jump rings:
Making Memories
Paper: Making Memories
Other: Foam board

how to: To emphasize Colton's handwriting,
Heidi made a window in foam board for
his writing sample and created a small
accordion-fold book for more lettering
and photos. Attach the Eyelet Tag
Alphabet with jump rings.

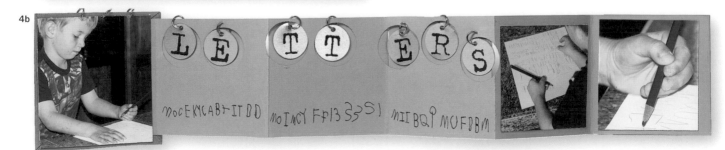

1 BLESSED
By Kris Stanger

Buttons, eyelet letters, funky with fiber, and scrapbook stitches: Making Memories
Computer font: Angelina
Paper: Making Memories and Dèjá Views
Vellum: Making Memories
Other: Chalks, fabric, pearls, and ribbon

how to: *With several pictures of her son and daughter together, Kris has the challenge of making the layout feminine and masculine. Her solution? Kris simply creates a double-page spread, putting her daughter's photos on one page with the feminine paper and putting her son's photos on the opposite page with masculine paper. By using the same color scheme on both sides, Kris can easily scrapbook her children's photos.*

2 ROMANCE
By Heidi Swapp

Brads, eyelet letters, eyelets, safety pins, and scrapbook stitches: Making Memories
Paint: Folk Art
Paper: Making Memories
Other: Currency from the Cayman Islands

how to: *Cut out leaf shapes from the top layer of dark blue cardstock so the light blue paper will show through. Wet, crinkle, and iron the paper to get a distressed effect. Accent the cutouts with a mixture of blue and white acrylic paint. Attach a silk flower with a large brad and dab a little blue paint on each. Stitch the corners of the photos down. For the title, attach each letter with a different treatment: safety pins, eyelets, brads, or jump rings.*

3 ZACHARY TY
By Erin Terrell

Alphabet stamps: PSX Design
Brads, eyelet charms, eyelet letters, eyelets, metal-rimmed tags, scrapbook stitches, and snaps: Making Memories
Embossing powder: Ranger Industries
Faux wax stick: Surebonder
Paper: Making Memories, Mustard Moon, and Creative Imaginations
Pens: EK Success
Stamping ink: Clearsnap and Tsukeniko
1/4" eyelets: Stamp Antonio
Other: Ribbon

how to: *To create the journaling blocks, tear and roll the top edge of white card-stock. Edge the white journaling block with an inkpad. For the heart tag, melt white wax on each circle tag. Dip a heart snap into an inkpad, then use the snap as a stamp to create a heart image in the melted wax. Adhere the Eyelet Letters with adhesive dots and adhere the title tags with colored snaps. Heat emboss a heart Eyelet Charm with white embossing powder, then use adhesive dots to secure it to your main photo. For the main photo on the right-hand side of the layout, set colored brads in each corner of the photo mat. Wind Scrapbook Stitches around each brad to create a frame. Erin's tip: Mix black and white photos with color photos for a fun, new look.*

4 FLOWER GIRLS
By Jennifer Jensen

Alphabet stamps: PSX Design
Beads, eyelet letters, and scrapbook stitches: Making Memories
Embossing enamel: Ultra Thick Embossing Enamel, Suze Weinberg
Embossing powder: Stampin' Up! and Top Boss
Fabric: American Folk & Fabric
Fiber: On the Surface
Flower petals: Rubba Dub Dub, Art Sanctum
Flowers: Hirshberg Schutz & Co.
Paint: Delta
Paper: Making Memories
Photo corners: Canson
Stamping ink: Clearsnap
Other: Beads, button, chain, hook, mat board, rhinestones, and tulle

how to: *After sewing fabric to the page, heat emboss the corners and edges of 12" x 12" paper with Ultra Thick Embossing Enamel. Then heat emboss on top of that with ivory powder and stamp the edges with a copper inkpad. Jennifer also heat embossed the edges of the photos with gold embossing powder. Paint the Eyelet Letters and small flowers with acrylic paint, then swipe the edges with a copper inkpad. Glue rhinestones on the letters or sew beads around the individual letters. Hand stitch the letters to your layout, sliding beads through the floss. Jennifer removed the top of several of the Eyelet Letters to make a chain for the letter "w."*

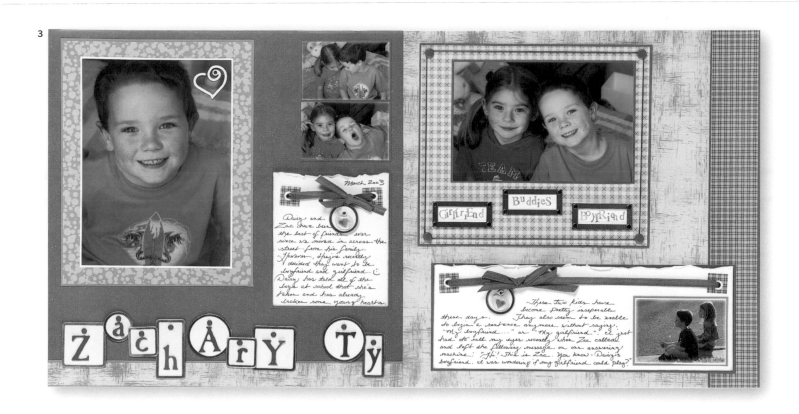

1 OBSESSION
By Emily Waters

Defined stickers, jump rings, metal words, mini-brads, snaps and staples: Making Memories
Paint: Folk Art
Paper: Making Memories
Square metal ring: Seven Gypsies
Walnut ink: Postmodern Design
Other: Fabric swatches and ribbon

how to: *Create a photo mat by taping off a rectangular section of your paper. Paint inside the taped-off area. Remove the tape and tear around the edges, leaving a slight border. Using a micro-hole punch, punch a hole in each Metal Word and use jump rings to connect all the words together, creating a frame around your photo. Set the photo mat in all four corners using screw snaps. Trim your photo to fit inside the Metal Word frame and attach both to the painted mat. Print out the word "obsession" and tear around the outside edges. Tie black and white gingham ribbon around a square metal ring. Adhere the ring around the "O" with Metal Glue. On the adjacent page, tear a piece of cream cardstock and adhere down the right side of oatmeal-colored cardstock. Place a strip of ribbon around the torn border. Fold walnut-inked cardstock over red fabric swatches and secure with a staple. Adhere swatches down the side of the page. Mount photos in desired areas and attach Defined Stickers with mini-brads.*

2 DREAM CANDLE
By Emily Waters

Handmade paper: Earthmade Papers
Defined sticker, eyelet charms, eyelet words, mini-brads, tiny straight pins, twistel and wire word: Making Memories
Other: Ribbon

how to: *Tear a 2 1/2" piece of black handmade paper and wrap it around the candle. Wrap a piece of ribbon around the top of the black paper and tie in the front. Place a portion of the Defined Sticker behind a tag Eyelet Charm. Place on candle and push brads into the candle through the four corners of the charm. Attach Wire Word to the candle using tiny straight pins, making sure the heads of the pins are holding down a section of the Wire Word. Trim the bottom off a tag Eyelet Charm and attach the Eyelet Word. String the tag onto Twistel and wrap it around the candle over the ribbon.*

3 TOGETHERNESS BOOK
By Emily Waters

Eyelet letters, eyelets, jump rings, metal frame, metal word, metal-rimmed tags, and simply stated rub-ons: Making Memories
Paper: Daisy D's
Other: Bolts, eye screws, ribbon, round metal washer, and wing nuts

how to: *Cut a front and back cover from a cardboard box. Trim the Metal Word between the "together" and the "ness." Place the "together" portion on top of your book cover and trace a rectangle around it with a straight edge. Using an X-Acto knife, cut out the hole from the cover. Use the same steps to create a hole for your photo. Attach the "ness" part of the word on the front cover just to the left of your cutout hole. Sand the front of a Metal Frame to rough it up so the paint will adhere. Paint the frame with acrylic paint. Once the frame is dry, use sandpaper or steel wool to scratch off some of the paint. Adhere a "moments" Simply Stated Rub-On to the side of the frame. Cut the frame in two corners and attach an eyelet on each of the four sides. Reposition the frame with jump rings through the eyelets. Adhere the frame around the cutout window on the front cover. Wrap a piece of ribbon around the front cover, tying the knot on the front. Slip on the circle washer. Attach the "4" Eyelet Letter to the black metal-rimmed tag with a jump ring, then tie onto the frame with a small piece of ribbon. Using a sharp hole punch, punch holes through the front and back cover and filler pages. Bind the book with bolts and wing nuts. Place the "together" portion of the Metal Word and a picture on the first page of your book. Attach tiny eye screws into the side of the front and back cover and tie a ribbon through each one to close the book.*

4 VALENTINE
By Stephanie McAtee

Adhesives: PVA, Paper Source; Mod Podge, Plaid
Alphabet charms, bead chain, and metal word: Making Memories
Alphabet stamps: PSX Design
Dried flowers: Pressed Petals
Flower stickers and small label: Anima Designs
Paint: Americana
Paper: Making Memories
Rubber stamps: Anna Griffin
Rub-ons: Craf-T Products
Other: Chipboard, galvanized steel, heart charm, and ribbon

how to: *Cut a piece of chipboard to size. Score and fold two sides in so they meet in the middle. Press down the folds with a bone folder to flatten. Open and lay flat. Measure cardstock to cover the outside of the card and allow extra to fold over to the inside. Adhere with PVA, smoothing out any wrinkles with a brayer. Let dry. Finish the inside by gluing a contrasting paper to cover the raw edges. Embellish with Eyelet Words, Alphabet Charms, and found objects. Tie closed with ribbon and a bead chain.*

5 CREATE A BABY
By Rhonda Solomon

Alphabet charms, buttons, charmed plaques, eyelet charm, snaps, and wire words: Making Memories
Alphabet stamps: Hot Potato and PSX Design
Mesh: Magenta
Paper: Making Memories
Photo corners: Boston International Inc.
Stamping Ink: Clearsnap
Other: Embossing powder

how to: *Color-block the background. Mat the main photo with black mesh and attach to the page with snaps. Tack Wire Words down with a needle and thread. Stamp "BABY" and heat emboss. Stamp the date on an Eyelet Charm and secure to the layout. Rub the edges of the paper with a white inkpad.*

5 charmed frames & charmed photo corners

Jenny Jerome Churchill commented, "Treat your friends as you do your pictures and place them in their best light." On a scrapbook page or project, you can place your friends and family in their best light with Charmed Frames™, which can be used in many innovative ways. For example, turn collaged frames into magnets to make a magnificent gift, ingeniously frame knobs on a key holder, or turn them into interactive, hinged embellishments.

Charmed Photo Corners™ are also perfect for highlighting your photos. Try putting the corners directly on your photos to help spotlight beautiful scenery. Or combine a photo corner with a corner made from vintage paper for added flair.

However, don't just think you have to use the frames and corners as they come! Notice how several artists altered the look of these products by painting, heat embossing, decoupaging, or covering them with mesh. With so many options, you're sure to find a style of Charmed Frames and Charmed Photo Corners to complement your photo or enhance the mood of a project to create a gallery of beautiful art.

1 MAGNET FRAMES
By Heidi Swapp

Adhesive: Mod Podge, Plaid
Charmed frames, charmed photo corners, defined stickers, and wire: Making Memories
Dried flowers: Nature's Pressed
Ribbon: Bucilla
Stickers: Wordsworth
Other: Concho, flower charm, foam board, magnets, postage stamps, and silver frame

how to: *Cut words from Wordsworth stickers and Defined Stickers. Arrange on Charmed Frames. Embellish with more collage elements such as postage stamps, dried flowers, ribbons, charms, and smaller decorative frames. Cover with Mod Podge. Cut pieces of foam board to the size of the frames. Put a photo on top of the foam board. Frame each photo with an embellished Charmed Frame. Adhere magnets to the back of the foam board. Stick to any metal surface for a personalized decoration!*

2 CORY BIRTHDAY CARD
By Heidi Swapp

Bead chain, charmed frame, charmed photo corner, metal-rimmed tag, page pebble alphabet, and star charm: Making Memories
Colored pencils: Prismacolor
Paint: Folk Art
Paper: Making Memories
Ribbon: Bucilla

how to: *Cut a strip from 12" x 12" paper to fit the width of your desired envelope. Fold the top down about 2" over a contrasting paper. Punch two holes in the flap for the ribbon tie. Cover a Charmed Frame with blue paint and allow to dry. Cover with cream-colored paint and allow to dry. Rub with steel wool to expose some metal and blue paint. Adhere a Charmed Photo Corner and Page Pebble Alphabet letters to the frame. Heidi trimmed the Page Pebbles so they would fit on the frame. Cut a hole in the envelope to expose the frame.*

3 BLUE-EYED GIRL
By Heidi Swapp

Alphabet charms, charmed frames, and charmed photo corners: Making Memories
Dried flowers: Nature's Pressed
Paper: Making Memories and Daisy D's
Ribbon: Bucilla
Stickers: Wordsworth
Other: Lace

how to: *Use postage stamps, dried flowers, ribbon, small Alphabet Charms, and cut-up stickers to decorate Charmed Frames. Use them to frame small pictures or Alphabet Charms.*

CHARACTER is the architecture of the being. -LOUISE NEVELSON

September 2002

1 CHARACTER
By Kris Stanger

Antiquing gel and paint: Delta
Charmed frames, and snaps:
Making Memories
Computer fonts: Book Antique and Codex
Fiber: On the Surface
Frame: My Mind's Eye
Hinges: Darice
Paper: Making Memories
Rubber stamp: Inkadinkado
Stamping ink: Stampin' Up!
Other: Eyelets, mesh ribbon, and
mulberry paper

how to: Rub tole paint on the Charmed
Frames with your finger, then rub a light
coat of antiquing gel over the top for a
rustic look. Attach them to your layout
with hinges.

2 M BABY BOOK
By Rhonda Solomon

Alphabet charms, charmed frame, and
eyelet word: Making Memories
Photo corners: Boston International Inc.
Other: Leaves, ribbon, and silk flowers

how to: Triple-mat a photo on sage green,
kraft-colored, and black cardstock. Make
some mats wide and some skinny. Place
a Charmed Frame over the photo. Add
photo corners to the black mat. Adhere
the Alphabet Charm and Eyelet Word in
place. Hot glue ribbon around the entire
album and tie closed. Adhere the photo
mat, flowers, and leaves on the front of
the album over the ribbon. Replace filler
pages with your choice of cardstock to
make a personalized album.

3 FRIENDS FOREVER
By Julie Turner

Computer font: Sylfaen, WordPerfect
Charmed frames, eyelet shapes, eyelets,
funky with fiber, and snaps:
Making Memories
Paper: Perspectives, Making Memories
Powdered pigment: Pearl-Ex, Jacquard
Products
Other: Fabric

how to: Cut fabric into strips and fray
the edges. Weave the strips together,
adhering the ends to the back of the
paper. Attach an Eyelet Shape to each
corner of the opening to highlight the
photo. The weaving and wrapping
emphasize the fact that the page
is in layers.

Rub Perspectives paper with Pearl-Ex
to give it more of a custom look. Use
fabric behind the openings to draw
attention to the cutouts. Adhere the
framed photos to the fabric and
embellish with snaps and fiber.

4 HAPPY BIRTHDAY
GIFT CARD AND BAG
By Rhonda Solomon

Alphabet stamps: PSX Design
Charmed frame: Making Memories
Embossing enamel: Ultra Thick Embossing
Enamel, Suze Weinberg
Embossing ink: Ranger Industries
Fibers: Timeless Touches
Paint: Delta
Stamping ink: Clearsnap

how to: Rubber stamp a leaf image on
a square of cardstock. Stamp "happy
birthday" over the top of the leaf. Rub
acrylic paint on a Charmed Frame.
Adhere the frame around the stamped
image with Metal Glue. Trim around the
frame, leaving a small border. Ink the
edges of the cardstock square. Place on a
small, dark green cardstock card and tie
at the top with a fiber bow. Adhere the
card to a gift bag. Heat emboss the
frame, stamped image, and part of the
bag with a clear embossing pad and
embossing enamel.

5 KEYS
By Rhonda Solomon

Alphabet charms, charmed frames, and
metal-rimmed tags: Making Memories
Alphabet stamps: PSX Design
Gel stain: DecoArt
Keys: Homestead Collectibles
Knobs and hooks: Precision Hardware
Paint: Delta
Primer: Kilz
Stamping ink: Clearsnap
Other: Ribbon

how to: Wash the front of a piece of
sun-bleached wood with a white gel
stain. Rub off. Apply primer to the brass
hooks. When dry, paint hooks with acrylic
paint. Let dry. On the top left side of the
board, hammer a small hook to hang
vintage-looking keys. Glue four Charmed
Frames at the top of the board. Let dry,
then drill holes for the knobs. Attach
knobs. With an electric drill, screw on
hooks below each frame. Stamp words
with silver ink on black metal-rimmed
tags. Hang tags on the knobs with
ribbon. Glue Alphabet Charms down
the right side.

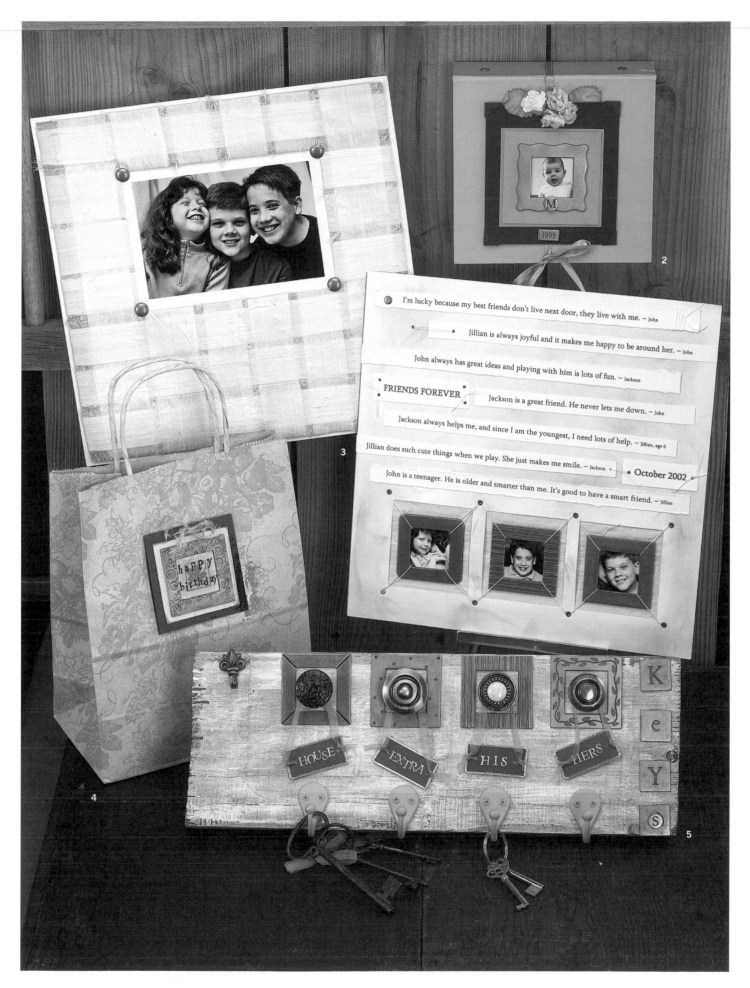

I'm lucky because my best friends don't live next door, they live with me. — John

Jillian is always joyful and it makes me happy to be around her. — John

John always has great ideas and playing with him is lots of fun. — Jackson

FRIENDS FOREVER

Jackson is a great friend. He never lets me down. — John

Jackson always helps me, and since I am the youngest, I need lots of help. — Jillian, age 6

Jillian does such cute things when we play. She just makes me smile. — Jackson

October 2002

John is a teenager. He is older and smarter than me. It's good to have a smart friend. — Jillian

happy birthday

1995

KEYS

HOUSE   EXTRA   HIS   HERS

1 WIMBERLY, TEXAS
By Erin Terrell

Alphabet charms, charmed frames, and charmed photo corners: Making Memories
Paper: Making Memories
Pens: EK Success
Watercolor paper: Strathmore
Watercolors: Loew-Cornell

how to: *Paint blues and greens on watercolor paper and adhere to the background paper. Mat and place photos as shown. Frame small photos with Charmed Frames. Add Charmed Photo Corners to focal photos and add Alphabet Charms to the main photo to create a title. Journal with a complementary pen color.*

2 DISCOVER
By Stephanie McAtee

Adhesive: Mod Podge, Plaid
Alphabet stamps: PSX Design
Charmed photo corners and eyelet shape: Making Memories
Paint: Americana
Paper: Making Memories
Rectangular ring: Seven Gypsies
Ribbon: Paper Source
Snap: Dritz
Vintage art: FoofaLa
Walnut ink: Anima Designs
Other: Button covers, chipboard, and silk flower

how to: *To make the typewriter-looking keys, take the backs off button covers. Put a pop-dot in each one to give the letters height. With a circle punch the size of the button cover, punch circles from white cardstock. Rubber stamp each letter into the center of each circle using acrylic paint as your ink. Stick the circles onto the pop-dot, inside each button cover. When the letters are dry, cover with Mod Podge to give the letters a glossy feel.*

3 DISCOVER TOGETHER
By Robin Johnson

Alphabet stamps: PSX Design
Charmed frame, charmed photo corners, defined stickers, and snaps: Making Memories
Embossing enamel: Ultra Thick Embossing Enamel, Suze Weinberg
Mesh: Magic Mesh, Avant Card
Pens: EK Success
Stamping ink: Tsukineko
Walnut ink: Postmodern Design
Other: Compass button and watercolors

how to: *Put a piece of mesh on the Charmed Frame and on each Charmed Photo Corner. Trim to size. Press a watermark inkpad on top of the mesh, then sprinkle bronze embossing enamel on top. Heat-set. Letter on kraft-colored cardstock with a clear embossing pen. Heat-set the word with clear embossing enamel. Paint around the word with dark blue watercolor paints. Once dry, use a thin, light gray pen to trace on the left side of the letters for a shadow effect. Stamp the remaining words on the title block. Tear around the title and secure in place with snaps. For the other random words on the layout, cut words from Defined Stickers and ink the edges. Then cut each word apart and add random inking to make each letter unique.*

4 LOVE IT WHEN
By Jennifer Jensen

Beads: Crystal Components
Brad, charmed photo corners, eyelet charm, and wire: Making Memories
Calligraphy ink: Daler-Rowney
Embossing enamel: Ultra Thick Embossing Enamel, Suze Weinberg
Fiber: On the Surface
Paint: Delta
Paper: Making Memories and Paper Adventures
Perfect Pearls: Ranger Industries
Other: Button, calligraphy pen, patterned paper, ribbon, and tin ceiling tile corner

how to: *Tear openings in cardstock to make picture frames. Rub the frames with purple acrylic paint, then dust with Perfect Pearls. Rub purple paint onto the Charmed Photo Corners. Jennifer also glued a bead in the center of the raised flower Charmed Photo Corners. Heat emboss the tin ceiling corner with Ultra Thick Embossing Enamel for a glossier look.*

3

4

6 eyelet words, eyelet phrases & eyelet quotes

A Chinese proverb professes, "Words are the keys to the heart." With Eyelet Words™, Eyelet Quotes™, and Eyelet Phrases™, you'll be filled with ways to express yourself and open the door to your loved one's heart. When you've found the perfect words to capture your thoughts, simply use an eyelet setter to set these metal objects on a page, card, book, or other creative endeavor.

But before you set these eye-catching eyelets on your work of art, try painting, inking, sanding, or heat embossing the surface for a fresh look. Use a few Eyelet Words here and there to fill in the blanks in your journaling. You could even be bold and set an Eyelet Word directly on a photo. Try matting an Eyelet Quote with paper or raising it off the page with foam board to set it apart from the rest of your layout. Or put one in a shadow box to tie together and give meaning to your collection of objects. As you unlock the doors of creativity, let these products speak for you!

1 AUTUMN
By Robin Johnson

Defined stickers, eyelet quote, and ribbon: Making Memories
Embossing powder: Stampendous
Paint: Delta
Paper: Creative Imaginations
Rubber stamp: Hero Arts
Stamping ink: Clearsnap and Tsukineko
Other: Scrim

how to: *Press an inkpad onto the Eyelet Quote several times until it is covered with ink. Heat emboss with clear embossing powder. When it has cooled, paint the edges of the quote with acrylic paint. You may need two coats of paint.*

For the fabric mat, cut the fabric 1/2" wider on top, bottom, and right side and 1 1/2" longer on the left side. Fold the longer side over a photo and stitch around the fabric 1/8" outside your photo.

2 SHADOW BOX
By Robin Johnson

Charmed photo corners, defined stickers eyelet phrases, eyelet quote, eyelet words, and eyelets: Making Memories
Embossing powder: Stampendous
Nest: Joshua's
Paint: Delta
Rubber stamp: All Night Media
Stamping ink: Tsukineko
Other: Fabric, foam board, leaves, pine cone, shadow box, and waxed linen

how to: *To paint the metal pieces, brush paint across the metal, making sure the paint sinks into the letters. Gently wipe paint off the surface of the metal with wet wipes. The paint will remain in the letters. For the word "explore," brush an inkpad across a Defined Sticker. Cut out the word you want, then peel off the backing. Cut the word apart into individual letters and place on a tag, leaving a little space between each letter. For the script tag, write script across a tag, stamp your image, and rub an inkpad across the edges to age. Finally, heat emboss with clear embossing powder. For the shadow box, paint and sand edges. To prop up photos, leaves, and other objects, cut and layer several small pieces of foam board and adhere everything with adhesive dots.*

3 WONDER MINI-BOOK
By Robin Johnson

Embossing enamel: Stampendous
Embossing ink: Tsukineko
Eyelet quote, eyelet shapes, and eyelet words: Making Memories
Metallic rub-ons: Craf-T Products
Paper: Amscan
Ribbon: Offray
Tag: American Tag
Other: Lace heart and leaves

how to: *Cover a book with patterned paper. Tear varying sizes of solid cardstock to create corner accents. Add color to the metal pieces with metallic rub-ons. Heat emboss the Eyelet Quote and Eyelet Shape with a clear inkpad and embossing enamel.*

For the journaling on the inside page, draw a box for the outside edge of your text area. Draw another box that is 1/4" smaller. Pencil in your title words. Then draw lines inside the box for the journaling. Pencil in your journaling. Ink it all in, erase the pencil lines, and glue the leaves on top.

1 TEXAS RANGER MUSEUM
By Erin Terrell

Charmed frame, charmed photo corners, and eyelet words: Making Memories
Daisy: Sanook Paper Company
Fibers: Creative Imaginations
Paint: DecoArt
Paper: Making Memories, Emagination Craft, and Scrap Ease
Pens: EK Success
Punches: All Night Media, EK Success, and Marvy Uchida
Ribbon: Offray
Stamping ink: Tsukineko
Vellum: Dèjá Views

how to: Create a background with patterned and solid papers. Paint randomly on the green textured cardstock with a stiff paintbrush. Run fibers along the left and right borders of the page, adhering the ends to the back of the paper. Mat photos as shown, double-matting some on patterned papers. Punch flowers from various colors of cardstock. Paint the edges of some, then adhere them in the bottom corner. Cut strips of paper, paint around the edges, then journal on them before adhering to your layout. Rub an inkpad over the Charmed Frame, then adhere the frame with adhesive dots. Adhere the paper flower in the frame. Rub an inkpad over the Eyelet Words and Charmed Photo Corners to change their color. Hang knotted ribbon from the tops of two photos. Flatten the backs of the Eyelet Words, then adhere them to the ribbon with adhesive dots. You could also set the Eyelet Words through the ribbon, photo, and background papers.

2 DID I EVER TELL YOU?
By Lynne Montgomery

Alphabet stamps: PSX Design
Computer fonts: CK Constitution, *Creating Keepsakes*; Amery
Eyelet words, eyelets, and metal-rimmed tags: Making Memories
Paper: Making Memories
Stamping ink: Tsukineko
Other: Fiber

how to: Cut journaling blocks a bit smaller than the metal-rimmed tags. Set Eyelet Words on the journaling blocks. Adhere the block to the tag, then set a mini-eyelet in each hole. Mount photos. Lay everything out to determine where the larger eyelets and fibers should go. Set three eyelets on both sides of the top and both sides of the bottom of your background cardstock. Lace three coordinating fibers through the eyelets and through the tags. Lynne's tip: A good font size for your journaling is 16-point or a bit larger so your journaling is somewhat in proportion to the Eyelet Words. And if you have a lot of journaling, you can adhere journaling blocks to the back of the tags so you can flip them over and read more.

3a

3b

4 WHEN YOU WISH UPON A STAR
By Sharon Lewis

Alphabet stamps: PSX Design
Computer font: Harrington, Microsoft Word
Embossed gold moon: Manto Fev
Embossing ink: Top Boss
Embossing powder: Ranger Industries
Eyelet words: Making Memories
Jewelry tag: American Tag
Paper: Making Memories, Magenta, and ScrapEase
Rubber stamp: A Stamp in the Hand
Stamping ink: Clearsnap and Tsukineko
Other: Star box and star studs

how to: *Trace the lid on the back side of gold paper. Add an extra 3/4" all the way around. Cut out and notch each corner and indentation. Cover the back side of the paper star with a glue stick and glue to the top of the lid. Cut two strips of gold paper, each measuring 2" x 12". Glue the strips around the edges of the lid. Notch the corners and fold to the inside of the lid. Stipple the edges of the lid with ink and a stippling brush. Rubber stamp the following poem around the edge of the box lid: "Star Light, Star Bright, First Star I See Tonight. I Wish I May, I Wish I Might, Have the Wish I Wish Tonight." Stamp 12" x 12" black paper with gold script. Cut it into five 4" x 4 3/4" pieces (one for each point). Cover each piece with a glue stick, and adhere to the box, one point at a time, overlapping the ends. Notch the corners. Wrap 1/2" over the top edge and 1/2" under the bottom of the box. Lightly apply embossing ink and gold embossing powder to the bottom edge of the box. Heat-set. Print out a quotation, leaving space around the words. Cut out each word individually and shade with brown ink. Cut brick-colored paper to size. Edge with gold ink. Glue on printed words and set Eyelet Words. Layer over torn, shaded script paper. Rubber stamp a jewelry tag and shade with ink. Wrap the tag's string around the Eyelet Word. Embellish the rest of the lid with moon and star studs.*

3 PHOTOJOURNALISM FINAL
By Stephanie McAtee

Alphabet stamps: PSX Design
Brad, eyelet words, jump rings, magnetic date stamp, page pebble, and staples: Making Memories
Paint: Americana
Paper: Making Memories
Pen: EK Success
Stamp collector's protector sheet: U.S. Post Office
Other: Bulldog clips and film negative

how to: *Cut a contact sheet (photograph of negatives) into strips. Stick them inside a stamp collector's protector sheet, giving them the look of negatives in a negative holder. Attach the protector to a piece of cardstock to create a unique background.*

On the left side of the layout, Stephanie layered photos that were turned in for a photojournalism final. Embellish the photos with Eyelet Words and journaling.

4

1a

1b

1 DISCOVER FRANCE
By Heidi Swapp

Adhesives: Diamond Glaze, JudiKins; PVA, Books By Hand
Embossing enamel: Ultra Thick Embossing Enamel, Suze Weinberg
Defined stickers, eyelet phrase, label holder, and simply stated rub-ons: Making Memories
Map: Paper Source
Ribbon: May Arts
Rubber stamps: Inkadinkado, Paper Inspirations, Stampa Rosa, and Stampers Anonymous
Stamping inks: Clearsnap
Other: Foam board, mica, and an old book

how to: *Cover an old book with map paper using PVA and a brayer. Rubber stamp on the cover and apply the "discover" Simply Stated Rub-On. To alter the metal on the two Eyelet Phrases, hold the eyelet on the back with tweezers and rub the phrase across an inkpad. With the ink still wet, dip the phrase into embossing enamel and heat-set. Dip it once more and heat-set again. To create the inside housing for the little book, cut two pieces of foam board to the same size. Cut the middle out of both pieces. Glue the two pieces of foam board together and cover with paper. Glue to the inside of the book. Run a piece of double-sided tape along the back for the ribbon to stick to. You could also make two small holes in the back of the book and run the ribbon through the holes. To make the little book that fits in the foam board cutout, fold four different styles and types of papers in half. Machine stitch up the fold to bind. Add Defined Stickers to the cover of the mini-book and cover them with mica using Diamond Glaze. Rubber stamp on the mica.*

2 CHANGING SEASONS
By Julie Turner

Canvas for inkjet printers: Paris Business Products
Computer fonts: Typewriter, P22; Zapf Ellipt, WordPerfect
Eyelet phrase: Making Memories
Matte spray fixative: Krylon
Paper: Making Memories
Powdered pigment: Pearl-Ex, USArtQuest
Snap tape: Dritz
Other: Cotton canvas, dried leaf, and split rings

how to: *To make the vintage photos look different than the recent photo, Julie scanned the images, reduced their color saturation (to make them look like old hand-colored photos), and printed them on canvas paper made for inkjet printers. Reducing the color saturation also helps photos with different color schemes blend better when used on the same page. Sew the photo to your layout. Age the background canvas and paper by rubbing it with antique gold and bronze Pearl-Ex. Spray the paper with a fixative to prevent the powder from rubbing off. The section of canvas in the lower right-hand corner was painted with a mixture of Pearl-Ex and water. Julie layered two colors to give it a richer look. Hand cut a tag, write or type your journaling on it, and slip it behind one of the photos.*

2

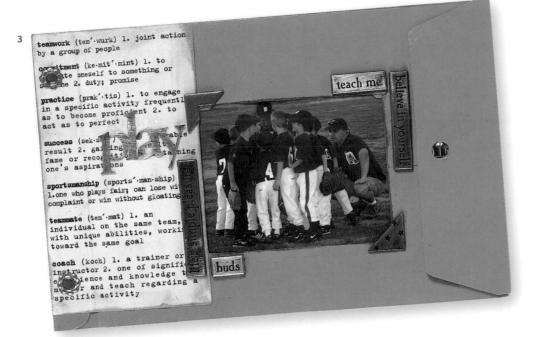

3

3 PLAY
By Heidi Swapp

Adhesive: Mod Podge, Plaid
Charmed photo corners, defined
stickers, eyelet phrases, eyelet words,
and metal word: Making Memories
Other: Eyelets and manila envelope

how to: *Cut 1/8" off the sides of an*
envelope. Cut the filler pages to the
correct size and secure in the bottom
end of the envelope with two eyelets.
Score the folds so the pages will turn
easily. Decoupage the cover to make
it sturdier. Embellish with Defined
Stickers. Heidi sanded the Eyelet
Phrases and Eyelet Words to give
them a new look.

4 MOTHERHOOD
By Heidi Swapp

Eyelet phrases and eyelet words:
Making Memories
Paper: Francis Meyer
Other: Lace, ribbon, and trim

how to: *To give the Eyelet Words and*
Eyelet Phrases a different look, rub
acrylic paint into the words, then wipe
the excess off with a wet wipe.

1 LOVIN' LIFE
By Kris Stanger

Antiquing gel and paint: Delta
Beads: Crystal Components
Dried flowers: Kris' own collection
Eyelet phrases, eyelet quotes, and snaps:
Making Memories
Fibers: On the Surface
Mesh: Magenta
Paper: Making Memories and Robin's Nest

how to: *Spring and summer are the perfect time for collecting wildflowers. Kris likes to save her old phone books and place the flowers between the pages. Set a heavy object on top of the book and leave them in the garage where it is warm and dry! Then you'll have the perfect page embellishment.*

2 SWEETEST FAMILY
By Julie Turner

Eyelet quote, eyelet shape, and wire:
Making Memories
Paper: Making Memories
Other: Glass and easel

how to: *Sandwich a photo and cardstock between two pieces of 1/4" thick glass. The glass was purchased and cut to size (4" x 6") at a local glass shop. The shop also ground the edges smooth. Use small adhesive dots to adhere the photo and cardstock to the back piece of glass. Use large adhesive dots to adhere the front piece of glass to the back piece. If your glue dots seem too big, just cut and use a small portion of one. The dots are hidden behind the Eyelet Quote and heart Eyelet Shape.*

3 MEGAN & JULIETTE
By Sharon Lewis

Alphabet stamps: PSX Design
Buttons, defined stickers, eyelet
quote, snaps, and scrapbook
stitches: Making Memories
Paper: Making Memories, Karen Foster
Design, and Sandylion
Poetry dog tags: Chronicle Books
Ruler: Limited Edition
Stamping ink: Clearsnap
Vellum: Making Memories
Other: Ribbon

how to: *Tear olive-colored patterned paper and adhere to brown cardstock. Roll the torn edge. Trim and mount photos. Rubber stamp names and titles on mat, first in brown ink, then again in black for a shadow effect. Tear or cut Defined Stickers, ruler, and music paper, and shade with an ink pad. Attach matted Eyelet Quote with snaps. Tie ribbons to dog tags and adhere with pop-up adhesive dots. Stitch buttons to the page.*

4 SENSE OF WONDER
By Heidi Swapp

Eyelet quote and staples:
Making Memories
Paper: Making Memories and
Karen Foster Design
Other: Foam board

how to: *Place a piece of foam board under the small photo and Eyelet Quote for added dimension. Rough up the quote with heavy-grit sandpaper.*

7 sheet metal, metal mesh & beyond

According to Webster, versatile is defined as "having many uses or applications." As such, it is the perfect word to describe Making Memories Sheet Metal™. It can be easily altered and tailored to fit your needs. The lightweight metal can be cut into shapes, embossed, folded, stamped, or painted to get the perfect look for your project. Pay attention to how you can frame cardstock with the metal or use it to cover a book. And don't be hesitant to stamp on it or use it as a background.

Just as versatile, Metal Mesh™ makes subtle corners for an entire page, not just a photo. Or you can hold a set of cards together with a length of mesh. If you're looking for a more feminine way to use the mesh, try painting it, then attach a magnet for a finishing touch. Experiment and use your ingenuity to see how many uses you can discover.

Now that several possibilities for metal products have been explored and showcased, here's a cornucopia of more creative ideas. Notice how the artists mix and match products and techniques to create memorable works of art.

1 PARTS OF EMILY
By Lynne Montgomery

Alphabet stamps: PSX Design
Bead chain, metal-rimmed tags, shaped clips, and sheet metal: Making Memories
Cotter pin and hinge: Seven Gypsies
Paper: Making Memories
Stamping ink: Ranger Industries
Other: Hat pin, metal coils, and ribbon

how to: *Cut cardstock into nine 3 1/2" squares. Cut nine 4 1/4" squares of Sheet Metal. Lay a square of cardstock in the center of a square of Sheet Metal. Score the edges. Fold each corner of metal onto the cardstock square. Next, fold each side of metal onto the square. Repeat the same steps for the remaining eight squares. Cut your photos with a circle punch and adhere to round metal-rimmed tags. Attach the tags to metal-wrapped cardstock with interesting hooks, pins, and chains. Finally, adhere all nine squares to a background piece of cardstock. Lynne's tip: Use a bone folder to flatten each fold of metal as you go. It helps make nice folds and sharp corners. The bone folder may scratch your metal, so if you don't want to see any scratches, flatten from the back side.*

2 LIFE: PUT YOUR HEART IN IT
By Lynne Montgomery

Alphabet charms, bead chain, brads, button, charmed photo corners, charmed plaque, eyelet alphabet, eyelet letters, eyelet shapes, eyelets, funky with fiber, metal-rimmed tags, page pebble, shaped clip, sheet metal, and snaps: Making Memories
Alphabet stamps: PSX Design
Computer font: CK Curly, *Creating Keepsakes*
Dried flowers: Nature's Pressed
Cotter pin and glass bottle: Seven Gypsies
Embossing tool: Lil' Boss, Paper Adventures
Hemp and waxed linen: Darice
Metal stamps: Pittsburgh
Paint: DecoArt and Plaid
Paper: Making Memories, Chatterbox, Colorbök, K & Company, Karen Foster Design, Penny Black, and Provo Craft
Poetry dog tag: Chronicle Books
Screen: American Art Clay Co. Inc.
Stain: Mini Wax Company
Stamping inks: Graphic Marker Inc. and Ranger Industries
Twine: May Arts
Other: Burlap, charms, clay leaf, green marble, microscope slides, mini-envelope, postage stamp, sand, and transparency

how to: *Find a box. According to Lynne, this is probably the hardest part of the project. Her box originally housed beads and had a Plexiglas cover. To make a new box look not so new, get a hammer and in Lynne's words, "Gently 'whack' away!" Next, stain the box. Then wash a little black paint around the edges. Lynne also used a little green paint here and there, as well.*

Choose a theme and color scheme and dig out all your favorite findings. You may need to drill holes in the box, as well. Do a general placement with some of your embellishments to see how everything will look. Then decorate one section at a time. Cut background papers, making sure they fit correctly in the spaces and adhere embellishments to them. Then adhere each background paper to the box. Think of each opening as an ultra-tiny scrapbook page.

3 BLESSINGS
By Lynne Montgomery

Alphabet stamps: PSX Design
Bead chain, metal-rimmed tag, and sheet metal: Making Memories
Computer font: CK Script, *Creating Keepsakes*
Dried flower: Nature's Pressed
Embossing tool: Lil' Boss, Paper Adventures
Paper: Making Memories and Karen Foster Design
Stamping ink: Ranger Industries
Other: Ribbon and transparency

how to: *Cover the front of a book or journal with Sheet Metal. Lynne used embossing tools to emboss three separate pieces of metal to use on the front. Adhere the embossed metal to the front of the covered book with photo tape. Lynne's tip: Use a sewing tracing wheel around the edges of your metal pieces for a stitched look.*

1 COASTAL DRIVE

By Heidi Swapp

Alphabet stamps: Barnes & Noble and
PSX Design
Brads and sheet metal: Making Memories
Dried flowers: Nature's Pressed
Paint: Folk Art
Paper: Making Memories and K & Company
Photo corners: Canson and Kolo
Ribbon: May Arts
Tag: American Tag
Walnut ink: Postmodern Design
Wire: Wire Art
Other: Trim

how to: *Heidi wanted the title to look
like an old metal sign, so she painted
it with both brown and green paint. To
create the title, use acrylic paint as your
stamping ink and rubber stamp on the
metal. Lightly outline the letters with a
black pen. To get the holes in the metal,
hammer a small nail into the metal and
run heavy wire through the two holes.
Paint white photo corners green to match
the layout. Crinkle and walnut ink the tag.*

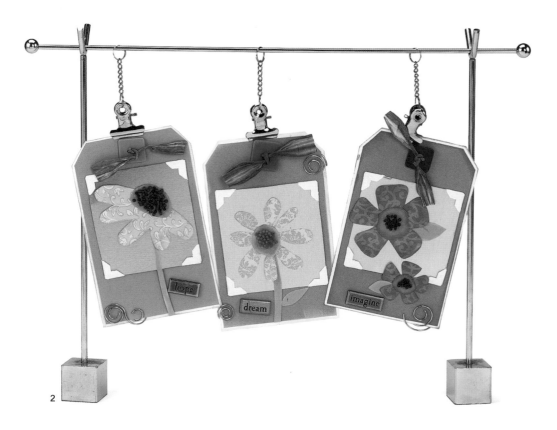

2 HOPE, DREAM, IMAGINE
TAG SERIES
By Rhonda Solomon

Beads, buttons, eyelet words, shaped clips, sheet metal, and twistel: Making Memories
Paper: Making Memories
Photo corners: Boston International Inc.
Stamping ink: Clearsnap

how to: *Cut tags from cardstock. Cut a metal square for the center of each tag. Adhere the metal to the tag with adhesive tabs. Cut a flower from printed paper. Add a piece of solid paper to create the center of the flower. Ink the edges of the flower and place on the metal square. Add a stem and/or leaf on each flower. Mat tags on white cardstock and ink the edges. Attach buttons to the tags with Twistel. Embellish with Eyelet Words, Shaped Clips, and photo corners.*

3 DRIVEN BY DEVOTION
By Erin Terrell

Charmed photo corner, eyelet shape, metal-rimmed tags, and sheet metal: Making Memories
Computer font: Carpenter ICG, downloaded from the Internet
Embossed stickers: Sharon Soneff, Creative Imaginations
Lettering template: Wordsworth
Paint: Americana
Paper: Making Memories and Magenta
Pen: Pentel
Photo paper: Photo Printasia Photo Satin Paper, Ilford
Ribbon: Offray
Vellum: Making Memories

how to: *Erin started this layout by reducing the hue and saturation of the photos in Photoshop, then printing them on photo satin paper. Create the bottom border with a strip of purple cardstock, tearing and rolling the top edge. Place embossed stickers along the bottom. Mat photos on green cardstock, then on patterned paper. Use a lettering template to create the "Driven by" part of title. Cut out with an X-Acto knife. Print the word "devotion" using the Carpenter ICG font. Cut out. Sew around the edges of white vellum, then adhere to the page with spray adhesive. Paint one Charmed Photo Corner with white paint. Cut words from the embossed stickers and adhere the words inside metal-rimmed tags. Cut a cross shape from Sheet Metal, then emboss random swirls within the cross. Adhere to your layout with adhesive tabs. Trace Charmed Photo Corners and a heart Eyelet Shape onto metal, then cut out the shapes. Emboss with swirls and adhere them to the photo and tag with adhesive dots. Journal on the page with a white gel pen.*

4 CRISSY
By Robin Johnson

Defined stickers and sheet metal: Making Memories
Rubber stamp: Hero Arts
Small leaf punches: Emagination Craft
Stamping inks: Anna Griffin and Stampa Rosa
Other: Large leaf punch, nameplate, and ribbon

how to: *To create the pressed tin look for the leaf border, punch shapes out of Sheet Metal and cardstock. Adhere the paper to the metal punches. Rub an inkpad across the edges of the paper/metal piece, adding extra random stroke marks. Glue to the background paper.*

1 REMEMBER
By Robin Johnson

Calligraphy ink: J. Herbin
Paint: Delta
Paper: Making Memories and
MM Colors by Design
Metal mesh and simply stated
rub-on: Making Memories
Stamp: Hero Arts
Stamping ink: Plaid
Other: Flower magnets and ribbon

how to: *Paint Metal Mesh with Delta
paint. Allow to dry or use an embossing
gun to quickly dry the paint. Adhere
the mesh with Metal Glue to the page
corners and add a flower magnet for
a feminine touch.*

2 THANK YOU CARD SET
By Heidi Swapp

Metal mesh, metal-rimmed tag, present
charm, shaped clip, and sheet metal:
Making Memories
Paper: Making Memories
Metal stamps: Pittsburgh
Other: Ribbon

how to: *Cut cardstock to 4" x 12". Fold
the side over 3". Punch a square in the
flap. Cut a piece of Metal Mesh to put
behind the hole and adhere with a dot
of glue. Use an adhesive dot to affix
the present charm in place. To hold the
cards together, fold a strip of mesh so
it will fit around all the cards. Stamp
the words "thank you" on a piece of
Sheet Metal, then wrap it around the
mesh for a final touch.*

3 ALL BOY
By Robin Johnson

Eyelet tag alphabet, jump rings, metal mesh, snap, and staples: Making Memories
Paper: Making Memories
String: DMC

how to: *Find two words with equal amounts of letters. Glue the coordinating letters together with Metal Glue. Cut the light blue paper to 7" x 10". Fold over 3" to create a panel. Cut three 1 1/4" squares out of the panel. Punch a micro-hole in the top center of each square. Attach the Eyelet Tag Alphabet letters to the card with jump rings. Hang alphabet tags in place. Next, cut a piece of dark blue cardstock to 7" x 11". Fold over 4". Position the dark blue on top of the light blue so the folded flaps meet in the middle. Add a screw snap to the outside edge of the light blue flap. Measure string or twine to wrap from the back of the card to the screw snap and to the back again. Glue or tape the string to the back of the dark blue paper. Glue the dark blue paper onto the light blue paper, hiding the attached twine. Cut a piece of Metal Mesh to fit the inside panel and secure in place with staples. Use the inside for photos and journaling.*

4 THE LEARNING PROCESS
By Heidi Swapp

Defined sticker, eyelet letter, metal mesh, and scrapbook stitches: Making Memories
Embossing enamel: Ultra Thick Embossing Enamel, Suze Weinberg
Paint: Plaid
Paper: Making Memories and SEI
Stamping ink: Tsukineko
Tag: Avery
Other: Alphabet stamps and ribbon

how to: *Paint the Metal Mesh with white paint. Allow to dry, then weave ribbon across the mesh. Bend the Metal Mesh over the bottom corner of the background paper. Paint and heat emboss the Eyelet Letter. Tie it to the mesh with ribbon and a tag.*

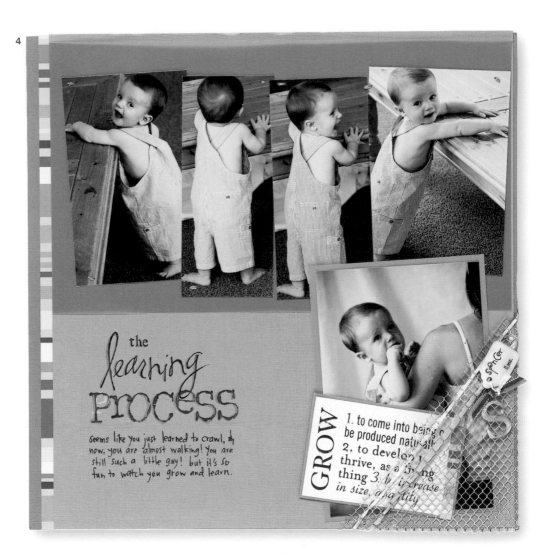

1 PRECIOUS LOVE
By Heidi Swapp

Adhesive: Diamond Glaze, JudiKins
Charmed frame, eyelet charm, eyelet
phrase, eyelet quote, eyelets, metal
word, and snaps: Making Memories
Paint: Plaid
Paper: Bazzill
Ribbon: May Arts and Midori

how to: *Paint the tag Eyelet Charm, Metal Word, and the Charmed Frames with acrylic paint. After they are dry, sand the surfaces until you achieve your desired look. Mount a Charmed Frame over an Eyelet Quote and glue in place. Put a photo under the other Charmed Frame. Adhere both frames to the page with Metal Glue and fill with Diamond Glaze. Allow to dry overnight. Dab the tops of the screw snaps with paint, as well.*

2 DISCOVER
By Emily Waters

Alphabet charms, charmed frames, defined stickers, eyelet phrases, eyelet words, and simply stated rub-ons: Making Memories
Jumbo eyelets: Dritz
Paint: Folk Art
Paper: Bazzill
Other: Patterned paper

how to: *Using sandpaper, rough up all the metal pieces to help the paint adhere better. Paint all the metal surfaces. Let dry, then paint a second coat and let dry. Once the paint is dry, lightly sand each piece with fine grit sandpaper. Trim two green strips of cardstock and sew around the edges. Adhere the sewn strips to the right side of each page. Sew around the green squares of paper, then adhere them to a strip of patterned paper. Affix photos to the squares and frame with Charmed Frames. Emily used jumbo eyelets to frame the Alphabet Charms in the word "discover." Simply hammer down the prongs on the back side of the eyelets and using Metal Glue, adhere the jumbo eyelets right on top of the Alphabet Charms. Use Defined Stickers and Simply Stated Rub-Ons for the page titles.*

3 GIRLFRIENDS
By Kris Stanger

Album, bead chain, eyelets, and metal word: Making Memories
Charms: No Boundaries
Paper: Making Memories
Other: Fiber and ribbon

hot to: *Apply adhesive to the vellum by running it through a Xyron machine. Affix it to the front of the album. Embellish the rest of the album with charms, decorative ribbon, and a Metal Word.*

4 JOURNAL
By Kris Stanger

Alphabet charms, charmed photo corners, magnetic date stamp, and shaped clips: Making Memories
Mesh: Magenta
Paper: Making Memories and KI Memories
Tags: Avery
Other: Cardboard, pencils, and ribbon

how to: *Cut thin cardboard for the covers of the journal. Cover and embellish the cardboard with assorted papers, mesh, Alphabet Charms, and Charmed Photo Corners. Insert filler paper between the covers and have it spiral bound at a copy store. Use the Magnetic Date Stamp to date the journal entry. Kris' tip. The patterned paper covering the journal is available in several other shades of the same pattern. This journal would make a great party favor if you made each girl's journal in a different shade. Wrap pencils with coordinating paper and finish off with ribbons and tags.*

4

1 SEASHELLS ARE TREASURES
By Kris Stanger

Alphabet charms, charmed plaques, and jump rings: Making Memories
Computer fonts: Angelina; Garamouche, P22
Paper: Making Memories and Kopp Design
Photo tinting dyes: Veronica Cas
Quotations: From Two Peas in a Bucket message board
Seahorse charm: The Card Connection
Stamping ink: Stamp Doctor
Other: Foam board, jute, seashell paper, and seashells

how to: *Place everything on your layout before you cut into the foam board. Leave enough space when you cut the paper so you can tuck the paper back behind your layout (on the cutouts). Use foam board so you can include mementos in your layout without smashing them or having a bulky layout. Kris used a 1/16" drill bit to make the holes in the Charmed Plaques. Use double-sided tape to adhere the sand to the terracotta-colored paper, making a natural background for the seashells.*

2 SUMMER
By Kris Stanger

Charmed photo corners, defined stickers, and eyelet letters: Making Memories
Flower eyelets: WooHooWowies!
Paper: Making Memories and Provo Craft
Raffia: Berwick
Seed beads: Mill Hill
Other: Chalk and mulberry paper

how to: *For a fun look, tear photos and mat on cardstock, leaving a narrow space in between the two pieces. Stitch beads along the middle of the tear.*

3 LITTLE GIRLS
By Jennifer Jensen

Charmed plaque and wire:
Making Memories
Calligraphy ink: Aladine
Flower: Hirschberg Schutz & Co.
Glass beads: Mill Hill
Paint: Accent
Paper: Making Memories and Doodlebug
Wide pink ribbon: Sheer Creations
Other: Buttons, small pink ribbon,
rhinestones, and textured paper

how to: *Rub pink acrylic paint over
the butterfly Charmed Plaque, then
glue cream beads in the holes of the
butterfly wings. Use buttons to "lift"
the plaque off the page.*

4 TIME IN A TIN
By Stephanie McAtee

Alphabet stamps: PSX Design
Defined stickers, eyelet tag alphabet, eyelets,
and page pebbles: Making Memories
Embroidery floss: DMC
Paint: Americana
Paper: Paper Source
Pocket watch rubber stamp:
Rubber Stampede
Slide frame: Manto Fev
Other: CD tin, Chinese coin, date
rubber stamp, fortunes, Kool-Aid,
watch parts, and a watch face cover

how to: *Cover a CD tin with acrylic
paint. Brush liquid Kool-Aid over the
top. Stephanie dried her tin with a heat
gun, which gave the tin a crackled look.
Make a mini-book to keep inside the tin.
Stephanie's book contains her thoughts
of motherhood and notes to her boys.
Affix a photo of yourself inside the lid
and use a date stamp to show when
you created the book.*

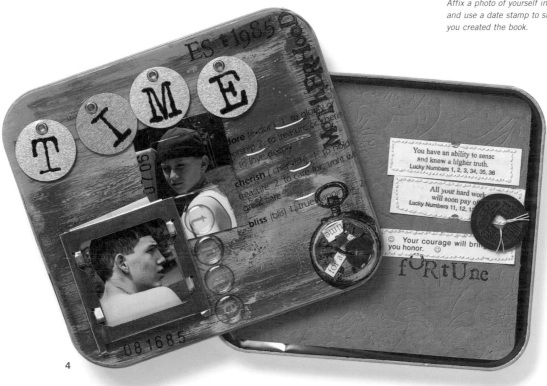

As artists, we were given the challenge to push ourselves to come up with innovative and fresh ways of working with metal on our creative projects. We loved altering the look of metal and expanding the possibilities for using metal embellishments. Now it is our chance to invite you to be inspired...beyond metal.

Erin Trimble

writer

Emily Waters

Julie Turner

Stephanie McAtee

Heidi Swapp

Sharon Lewis

Rhonda Solomon

Robin Johnson

Lynn Montgomery

Jennifer Jensen

Erin Terrell

Kris Stanger